Excel Basic Skills

Year 3

Ages 8–9

English

Get the Results You Want!

Donna Gibbs

PASCAL PRESS

Contents

Introduction

The aim of the ***Excel*** **Basic Skills English** series is to build on and reinforce students' basic skills in English. Each book in the series supports the requirements of Australian Curriculum English at each year level.

The ***Excel*** **Basic Skills English** series consists of seven books, one for each year level, from Kindergarten/Foundation to Year 6. The series is supported by other books in the ***Excel*** **Basic Skills** and **Advanced Skills** series.

Structure of the book

This book contains:

- thirty carefully graded, double-page units of teaching and learning activities
  - **Unit A** includes a sample informative, imaginative or persuasive text on subject matter relevant to a range of curriculum areas, and deals with **Reading and Comprehension skills.**
  - **Unit B** deals with the language conventions of **Spelling, Vocabulary, Grammar and Punctuation**.
- four double-page **revision units.**
- four double-page **NAPLAN-style Tests.**

How to use this book

- Students should complete one unit per week. A suggested plan would be to complete the Unit A page for the week on one day and the Unit B page on another day of the same week.
- At the end of a sequence of units students should undertake the applicable Revision units. If students find particular revision questions difficult they should revisit those areas in the previous sequence of units.
- After appropriate revision activities students should undertake the NAPLAN-style Test for those units. The revision work and testing should be completed on different days.

How to use this book with the *Excel* Basic Skills Mathematics series

For a complete **weekly English and Mathematics program** use this book in conjunction with the ***Excel*** *Basic Skills Mathematics Year 3* book. This way a student will have work set for four days a week—two days for English and two days for Mathematics.

How to assess students' progress

- Templates are included in each book of the series that outline the knowledge and skills targeted by the questions in that book. (Please see page 6.)
- The questions move through the subtopics of English in exactly the same order in each book but as there are more questions and more complex material included in later years of the Kindergarten/Foundation to Year 6 continuum, the question numbers vary across the books.
- The results of the work undertaken in each unit can be recorded on the marking grids. Please see the example on page 4. The marking grids on pages 6 and 7 are easy-to-use diagnostic tools that indicate where students' strengths and weaknesses lie in relation to specific areas of English. These results can be used to gather extra information about students' progress and their further revision needs.

The *Excel* Basic Skills and Advanced Skills series

If students are experiencing difficulty, require additional practice or need extension in any area of the course, further books are available to support them in the ***Excel*** **Basic Skills** and **Advanced Skills** series. (Please see the comprehensive list of ***Excel*** books on page 5.)

The *Excel* step-by-step improvement plan

Step 1

Read the introduction on page 3.

Step 2

Read this page, along with the marking grids and question templates on pages 6 and 7.

- **Question templates**
  These outline the knowledge and skills targeted by the questions in the book.
  Remember that the questions move through the subtopics of English in exactly the same order in each unit of the book.
- **Marking grids**
  The results of the work undertaken in each unit can be recorded on the marking grids.
  These are an easy-to-use diagnostic tool that indicate where each student's strengths and weaknesses are in relation to specific areas of English.
  These results can be used to gather extra information about each student's progress and their further revision needs. For example, see the sample marking grid in the right-hand column:
  - If a student is consistently getting more than one in five questions wrong in any topic they need help in this area.
  - When marking answers on the grid, simply mark incorrect answers with 'X' in the appropriate box. This will result in a graphical representation of areas needing further work. An example for the first five units is shown above. If a question has several parts, it should be counted as wrong if one or more mistakes are made.
  - Remember that you can identify what topics a student is having difficulty with by the number of questions they get wrong. For example, in the grid above the student is having difficulty with Reading and Comprehension inferring questions.

	Literal	*Literal*	*Literal*	*Inferring*	*Inferring*	*Evaluative*
Question	**1**	**2**	**3**	**4**	**5**	**6**
Unit 1				X		
Unit 2					X	
Unit 3						
Unit 4				X	X	
Unit 5					X	
Unit 6						
Unit 7						
Unit 8						
Unit 9						
Unit 10						

This grid indicates that the student needs extra help and practice in inferring questions.

Step 3

Refer to page 5 ***Excel* books to help you *get the results you want*!**

- Under each topic there is a comprehensive list of books in our range to help students.
  For example, if a student wants help with Reading and Comprehension inferring questions the books shown at the top of the next page will help them.
  Each ***Excel*** book has a comprehensive contents page that will help you find the appropriate pages in the book to target the specific topic you want in each subject area.

Excel books to help you *get the results you want!*

Reading and Comprehension

Excel Basic Skills

9781741251661

9781864412789

Excel Advanced Skills

9781741254525

Excel NAPLAN*-style Tests

9781741253634

9781741251722

Spelling

Excel Basic Skills

9781864412826

Excel Advanced Skills

9781741252606

Excel Handbooks and Guides

9781864410617

Excel NAPLAN*-style Tests

9781741253634

9781741251722

Vocabulary

Excel Basic Skills

9781864412826

Excel Basic Skills

9781741251630

Excel Advanced Skills

9781741252606

Excel NAPLAN*-style Tests

9781741253634

9781741251722

Grammar

Excel Basic Skills

9781864412840

Excel Advanced Skills

9781741253993

Excel Handbooks and Guides

9781864410600

Excel NAPLAN*-style Tests

9781741253634

9781741251722

Punctuation

Excel Basic Skills

9781864412840

Excel Advanced Skills

9781741253993

Excel NAPLAN*-style Tests

9781741253634

Excel NAPLAN*-style Tests

9781741251722

Writing

Excel Basic Skills

9781740200462

Excel Advanced Skills

9781741254037

General

Excel Basic Skills Core

9781864412741

Excel Basic Skills

9781741251562

Reading and Comprehension — QUESTION TEMPLATES

1–3 **Literal** Answers to these questions are found directly in the text.

4–5 **Inferring** Answers to these questions need to be worked out from clues in the text.

6 **Evaluative** Answers to this question rely on making judgements about information in the text and beyond the text.

Spelling

1–4 **Proofreading**
In these questions, students use their understanding of spelling patterns and spelling rules to correct the spelling mistakes.

5 **Word families**
In this question, students use their understanding of base words, morphemes, prefixes, suffixes and etymology to create word families.

Vocabulary

6–9 **Synonyms, meaning in context, definitions**
Students need to comprehend the meaning of words in context to answer these vocabulary questions.

10–11 **Antonyms**
Students need to understand synonyms and antonyms to answer these vocabulary questions.

Grammar

12 **Nouns/Noun groups**
This question deals with aspects of a noun group, e.g. nouns, adjectives and articles.

13 **Verbs/Verb groups**
This question deals with aspects of a verb group such as types of verbs, tense and subject–verb agreement.

14 **Adverbials**
This question deals with prepositional phrases and adverbs.

15 **Cohesion**
This question deals with ways to link ideas across a text, e.g. pronouns and conjunctions.

Punctuation

16–18 **Proofreading**
These questions deal with aspects of punctuation for different kinds of sentences, including quoted (direct) and reported speech.

Reading and Comprehension — MARKING GRID

	Literal	*Literal*	*Literal*	*Inferring*	*Inferring*	*Evaluative*
Question	**1**	**2**	**3**	**4**	**5**	**6**
Unit 1						
Unit 2						
Unit 3						
Unit 4						
Unit 5						
Unit 6						
Unit 7						
Unit 8						
Unit 9						
Unit 10						
Unit 11						
Unit 12						
Unit 13						
Unit 14						
Unit 15						
Unit 16						
Unit 17						
Unit 18						
Unit 19						
Unit 20						
Unit 21						
Unit 22						
Unit 23						
Unit 24						
Unit 25						
Unit 26						
Unit 27						
Unit 28						
Unit 29						
Unit 30						
Question	**1**	**2**	**3**	**4**	**5**	**6**

Conventions of Language

	Spelling					Vocabulary						Grammar				Punctuation		
	Proofreading	Proofreading	Proofreading	Proofreading	Word families	Synonyms	Synonyms	Meaning in context	Definitions	Antonyms	Antonyms	Nouns/ Noun groups	Verbs/ Verb groups	Adverbials	Cohesion	Proofreading	Proofreading	Proofreading
Question	**1**	**2**	**3**	**4**	**5**	**6**	**7**	**8**	**9**	**10**	**11**	**12**	**13**	**14**	**15**	**16**	**17**	**18**
Unit 1																		
Unit 2																		
Unit 3																		
Unit 4																		
Unit 5																		
Unit 6																		
Unit 7																		
Unit 8																		
Unit 9																		
Unit 10																		
Unit 11																		
Unit 12																		
Unit 13																		
Unit 14																		
Unit 15																		
Unit 16																		
Unit 17																		
Unit 18																		
Unit 19																		
Unit 20																		
Unit 21																		
Unit 22																		
Unit 23																		
Unit 24																		
Unit 25																		
Unit 26																		
Unit 27																		
Unit 28																		
Unit 29																		
Unit 30																		
Question	**1**	**2**	**3**	**4**	**5**	**6**	**7**	**8**	**9**	**10**	**11**	**12**	**13**	**14**	**15**	**16**	**17**	**18**

Reading and Comprehension

It's rugby for Rosie

Dear Diary

This week I am going to try out for the Under Nine District Rugby Team. I began playing rugby with my brothers when I was four and a half. Jem is already in the Under Twelve District Team. Bill likes playing rugby at the park with us when he doesn't have band practice. He plays the cello.

When I was seven I was chosen to be in our local rugby team, the Tireless Tigers. Tackling and passing are the things I like best. Dad helps me train during the week to keep up my fitness level.

I am a bit nervous about trying out for the district team. There are plenty of people who want to get into the team. The trials are on Saturday and all the family is coming. If I miss out I'm determined to try again next year. Wish me luck!

By Rosie

1. How old was Rosie when she began playing rugby?
   - **A** four
   - **B** four and a half
   - **C** seven
   - **D** eight

2. What part of rugby does Rosie like best?
   - **A** playing in the park
   - **B** getting fit
   - **C** tackling and passing
   - **D** trying out for teams

3. Who are the Tireless Tigers?
   - **A** Rosie's brothers
   - **B** the state team
   - **C** the Under Nine District Rugby Team
   - **D** the local team

4. How does Rosie's family feel about her playing rugby?
   - **A** pleased
   - **B** disappointed
   - **C** worried
   - **D** cross

5. Why is Rosie nervous about the trials?
   - **A** There is a lot of competition.
   - **B** She isn't very good at rugby.
   - **C** She isn't as good at rugby as her brother.
   - **D** She is nervous about everything.

6. How keen is Rosie to get into the district team?
   - **A** quite
   - **B** not very
   - **C** very
   - **D** fairly

Spelling

Rewrite the misspelt words.

1 Rosie wants to get into the district <u>teem</u>.

2 Rosie has a twin <u>bruther</u> named Bill.

3 I need to train twice a <u>weak</u>.

4 The whole <u>familly</u> went to the rugby.

5 Write three words that rhyme with **am**.

Vocabulary

Circle the word that has the nearest meaning to the underlined word.

6 She felt <u>nervous</u> in case she made a mistake.

A afraid B scared
C anxious D terrified

7 I am in the local team <u>already</u>.

A now B soon
C today D always

8 Add a word from the text to the sentence.

I hope I will be ______ for the team.

9 Write a word from the text to match the meaning.

being set on doing something

Circle the word on each line that does **not** belong.

10 low short high little

11 dislikes hates likes loathes

Grammar

12 Complete the sentence with a common noun from the text.

I have two ______.

13 Complete the sentence with an action (doing) verb from the text.

When Bill grows up he wants to ______ the cello in an orchestra.

14 Write a prepositional phrase from the text to tell **where**.

Bill likes playing rugby with us ______.

15 Choose a pronoun from the box to complete the sentence correctly.

he	she	it	you	they	I	we

Dad helps me to train because ______ wants me to be fit.

Punctuation

16 Circle the sentence that is punctuated correctly.

A She hopes to get into the district team the Super Seals.
B She hopes to get into the district team the Super Seals!
C She hopes to get into the district team, the Super Seals.

Rewrite each sentence correctly.

17 jem is good at rugby

18 ill be trying out next weekend

Reading and Comprehension

The ugly duckling

When Mother Duck's last egg finally cracked open, she was shocked.

'You don't look like my other ducklings,' she quacked. 'You are so big and ugly.'

The newborn duckling entered the pond with the other ducks but they soon made fun of him. They were so cruel and unkind that the sad, frightened duck ran away. Wherever he went from then on, he was badly treated.

Winter came and the ugly duckling found it hard to find food and shelter. Then one day he saw some beautiful birds circling high in the sky and felt a strange feeling. He wanted to join them but he was afraid. He hid his face under his wing.

To his surprise, the swans began to stroke his neck with their beaks as a welcome.

The duckling looked at his reflection in the stream. He was no longer an ugly duckling but a beautiful swan. His life had changed forever and for the better.

Retold from a story by Hans Christian Andersen

1. How did the mother duck feel when her last egg was hatched?
   - **A** scared
   - **B** sad
   - **C** frightened
   - **D** shocked
2. How did the mother duck describe the newborn duck?
   - **A** strange and beautiful
   - **B** cruel and unkind
   - **C** big and ugly
   - **D** sad and scared
3. Which season was most difficult for the duckling?
   - **A** spring
   - **B** summer
   - **C** autumn
   - **D** winter
4. Why did the other ducks make fun of him?
   - **A** He couldn't swim.
   - **B** He looked different from them.
   - **C** He made fun of them.
   - **D** They knew he was a swan.
5. 'He wanted to join them [the swans] but he was afraid.' Why?
   - **A** They were ugly.
   - **B** He thought they would be unkind to him.
   - **C** Their beaks were large and frightening.
   - **D** They looked strange.
6. Whose fault was it that the ugly duckling was so unhappy?
   - **A** his own
   - **B** nobody's
   - **C** the ducks'
   - **D** the swans'

Spelling

Rewrite the misspelt words.

1. The last duckling finaly broke from his egg.

2. Some animals are very crewel to each other.

3. The ugly duckling was badly treeted.

4. The swans gently stroked his neck with their beeks.

5. Write three words that rhyme with **un**.

Vocabulary

Circle the word that has the nearest meaning to the underlined word.

6. The young ducks frightened the newborn duckling.
   - **A** teased
   - **B** tricked
   - **C** scared
   - **D** shocked
7. The ugly duckling was astonished.
   - **A** surprised
   - **B** horrified
   - **C** envious
   - **D** shaken
8. Add a word from the text to the sentence.
   Without warm ________ the duckling could have frozen to death.
9. Write a word from the text to match the meaning.
   not pleasing in appearance ________

Circle the word on each line that does **not** belong.

10. difficult hard easy troublesome
11. frightened scared anxious contented

Grammar

12. Complete the sentence with a common noun from the text.
    Six ________ had already hatched.
13. Complete the sentence with an action (doing) verb from the text.
    When he felt shy he ________ his head under his wing.
14. Write a prepositional phrase from the text to tell **where**.
    The duckling looked at his reflection
    ________.
15. Choose a pronoun from the box to complete the sentence correctly.

he	she	it	you	they	I	we

The mother duck quacked, 'What an ugly duckling ________ are!'

Punctuation

16. Circle the sentence that is punctuated correctly.
    - **A** The ugly duckling was really a swan.
    - **B** The ugly duckling was really a swan?
    - **C** The ugly duckling was really a swan!

Rewrite each sentence correctly.

17. The sad frightened duck ran away from home

18. 'You are so big and ugly' she quacked.

Reading and Comprehension

Cooking an omelette

Utensils

- large bowl
- fork
- 20-cm non-stick frying pan
- spatula
- knife

Ingredients

- two eggs
- one tablespoon of milk
- seasoning (e.g. salt, pepper, herbs)
- one teaspoon of butter
- fillings such as chopped mushrooms, onions, tomatoes, ham, grated cheese

Method

Crack the shells of the eggs firmly and empty the eggs into the bowl. Add milk and lightly whisk with the fork to combine them. Add seasoning. Heat butter in a non-stick frying pan over medium-high heat. When butter starts to foam, add the mixture. Gently shake the pan to distribute it around. As eggs begin to cook around the edges, use the fork to draw the cooked part into the centre.

After 30 seconds, the eggs should be still soft but just set. Add fillings of your choice down the centre. Use the spatula to fold one side of the omelette over the filling. Then slide the omelette onto a plate fold-side down.

1. How do you crack the eggs?
   - **A** gently
   - **B** quickly
   - **C** firmly
   - **D** softly

2. How do you whisk the eggs?
   - **A** lightly
   - **B** suddenly
   - **C** smoothly
   - **D** briskly

3. What do you use to fold the omelette over?
   - **A** fork
   - **B** spatula
   - **C** frying pan
   - **D** bowl

4. What sort of omelette is being cooked?
   - **A** ham
   - **B** cheese
   - **C** your choice of ingredients
   - **D** mushroom

5. What makes this a healthy meal?
   - **A** It includes milk.
   - **B** It includes eggs.
   - **C** It includes vegetables.
   - **D** It only includes healthy ingredients.

6. The language used in this recipe is mostly
   - **A** striking and vivid.
   - **B** witty and funny.
   - **C** matter-of-fact.
   - **D** affectionate.

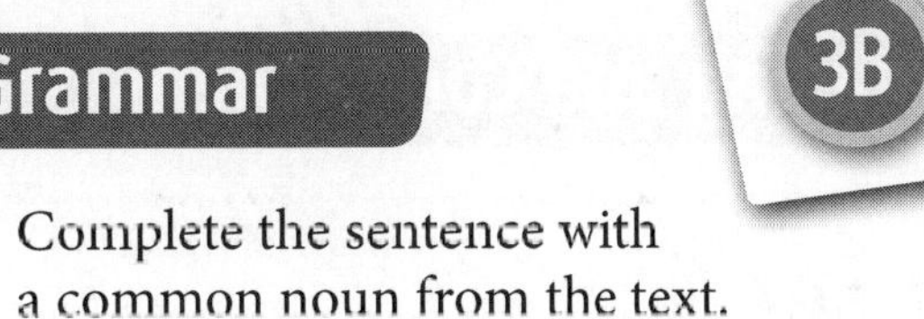

Spelling

Rewrite the misspelt words.

1 He choped some mushrooms for his omelette.

2 Put the eggs in the bowel.

3 You need to drawer the egg towards the middle of the pan.

4 If you heet the plate it will keep the eggs warm.

5 Write three words that rhyme with **ake**.

Vocabulary

Circle the word that has the nearest meaning to the underlined word.

6 She slid the omelette onto a plate.

A pushed B pulled
C slipped D threw

7 I don't have the right utensils for cooking.

A bowls B forks
C knives D equipment

8 Add a word from the text to the sentence.
Mum uses ______ rather than salt and pepper to season her cooking.

9 Write a word from the text to match the meaning.
a combination of things ______

Circle the word on each line that does **not** belong.

10 begins starts ends commences

11 firmly weakly gently softly

Grammar

12 Complete the sentence with a common noun from the text.
My favourite filling is ______.

13 Complete the sentence with an action (being) verb from the text.
When butter is heated it begins to ______.

14 Write a prepositional phrase from the text to tell **where**.
Crack the eggs and empty them ______.

15 Choose a pronoun from the box to complete the sentence correctly.

he	she	it	you	they	I	we

I cooked breakfast for Mum and Dad and ______ said it was delicious.

Punctuation

16 Circle the sentence that is punctuated correctly.

A Mum likes her omelette with ham cheese mushroom and onion.
B Mum likes her omelette with ham, cheese, mushroom and onion.
C Mum likes her omelette with ham, cheese, mushroom and onion?

Rewrite each sentence correctly.

17 if the heat is too high, youll burn the eggs.

18 Its easy to poach an egg

Reading and Comprehension

Insects

Ms Wood: Get your magnifying glasses, please. We are going outside into the playground to study insects. Any questions before we go?

Jimmy: How do you know something is an insect?

Ms Wood: You can recognise insects by looking closely at their bodies. They have six legs, three body parts (head, thorax and abdomen) and a single pair of antennae on their head. They usually have wings.

Scarlet: How many insects are there in the world?

Ms Wood: Scientists estimate there are around ten quintillion (10 000 000 000 000 000 000) insects moving around our planet! Over a million different species have already been discovered.

Bill: Are they any use?

Ms Wood: Yes, Bill. They are a very important part of our food chain. Think of the importance of pollination by bees, for example. Insects do far more good than they do harm.

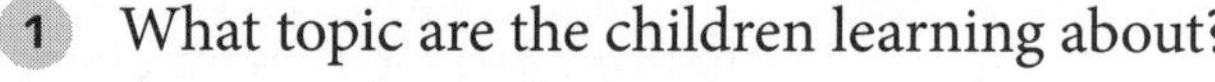

1. What topic are the children learning about?
   - A magnifying glasses
   - B scientists
   - C insects
   - D bodies

2. How many body parts does an insect have?
   - A six
   - B three
   - C one
   - D two

3. How many insects are there on our planet?
   - A around 10 000 000 000 000 000 000
   - B around 10 000 000 000
   - C 10 000 000 000 000 000 000 000
   - D 10 000 000 000 000 000

4. Where is this conversation taking place?
   - A in the playground
   - B outside
   - C in a classroom
   - D in a kitchen

5. What will the magnifying glasses be used for?
   - A burning leaves
   - B looking closely at insects
   - C looking at bees
   - D games in the playground

6. Are the children likely to find insects in the playground? Give reasons for your answer.

Spelling

Rewrite the misspelt words.

1 An example of an insekt is the bee.

2 Did you ask me a qestion?

3 Bring your magnifying glases over here, please.

4 Insects have a single pear of antennae.

5 Write three words that rhyme with **ink**.

Vocabulary

Circle the word that has the nearest meaning to the underlined word.

6 Stick insects are usually hard to find.

A strangely B never
C always D often

7 Many new species of insect have been discovered.

A detected B noticed
C found D seen

8 Add a word from the text to the sentence.

Scientists ______ that more species of insect will be discovered.

9 Write a word from the text to match the meaning.

jointed feelers found on the head of an insect

Circle the word on each line that does **not** belong.

10 inside interior outside indoors

11 important useless unimportant worthless

Grammar

12 Complete the sentence with a common noun from the text.

I saw a stick ______ hanging on the wall.

13 Complete the sentence with an action (being) verb from the text.

Insects ______ much more good than harm.

14 Write a prepositional phrase from the text to tell **where**.

Insects' antennae are located ______.

15 Choose a pronoun from the box to complete the sentence correctly.

he	she	it	you	they	I	we

She saw the insect and took a photo of ______.

Punctuation

16 Circle the sentence that is punctuated correctly.

A are there more insects than people on our planet?
B Are there more insects than people on our planet.
C Are there more insects than people on our planet?

Rewrite each sentence correctly.

17 spiders arent insects

18 This bug has six legs three body parts and two antennae

Reading and Comprehension

Canberra

In January 1901, the Australian colonies joined together to form the Commonwealth of Australia. As Australia was a new nation it needed a capital city of its own.

There was much disagreement about where the new capital should be. Some argued it should be in a cold part of the country so the men who governed could think clearly! Others pointed out it should not be near the coast. It would be at risk of invasion there.

Australians were asked to suggest names for the new capital. Among the suggestions were Eucalypta, Kangaremu, Thirstyville, Cookaburra, Canberra and Sydmeladperbrisho. Canberra, a name meaning 'meeting place' in the local Aboriginal language, was the final choice.

Canberra now has a strikingly modern parliament house on a lake and several significant museums, including the National Portrait Gallery. It is affectionately known as the bush capital.

1. What happened in Australia in January 1901?
   - **A** A new capital city was chosen.
   - **B** The Commonwealth of Australia was formed.
   - **C** Canberra turned 100.
   - **D** The states were invaded.

2. Why did Australia need a capital city?
   - **A** People were tired of the old capital city.
   - **B** It had gained more people.
   - **C** It was a colony.
   - **D** It was a new nation without a capital.

3. What does the name Canberra mean?
   - **A** capital city
   - **B** Aboriginal land
   - **C** meeting place
   - **D** head of state

4. The word 'Sydmeladperbrisho' is made up of the shortened names of
   - **A** capital cities.
   - **B** states.
   - **C** animals.
   - **D** people.

5. Which of these ideas are out of date? Choose all that apply.
   - **A** Only men should govern.
   - **B** Nations need a capital city.
   - **C** Taking risks can be unwise.
   - **D** Men only think well when it's cold.

6. What does the author think of Canberra as a city?
   - **A** impressive
   - **B** ordinary
   - **C** old-fashioned
   - **D** unimpressive

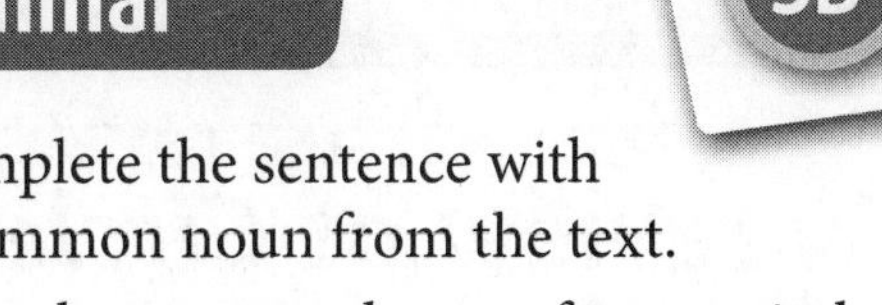

Spelling

Rewrite the misspelt words.

1 Australia became a nashion.

2 Canberra is a long way from the coste.

3 Dissagreement between the states was a problem.

4 Canberra makes a fine capitol city.

5 Write three words that rhyme with **ame**.

Vocabulary

Circle the word that has the nearest meaning to the underlined word.

6 They made a choice eventually.
A soon B finally
C later D afterwards

7 The old parliament house has been replaced by a modern one.
A old-fashioned B handsome
C up-to-date D out-of-date

8 Add a word from the text to the sentence.
Canberra is the capital city of ________.

9 Write a word from the text to match the meaning.
difference of opinion ________

Circle the word on each line that does **not** belong.

10 significant important useful noteworthy

11 affectionate loving unfriendly warm-hearted

Grammar

12 Complete the sentence with a common noun from the text.
Is Canberra a good name for a capital ________?

13 Complete the sentence with an action (being) verb from the text.
The states ________ together to form a nation.

14 Write a prepositional phrase from the text to tell **where**.
The new parliament house is ________.

15 Choose a pronoun from the box to complete the sentence correctly.

he	she	it	you	they	I	we

Canberra has a modern parliament house and ________ is on a lake.

Punctuation

16 Circle the sentence that is punctuated correctly.
A Canberra is a lively modern attractive capital city!
B Canberra is a lively, modern, attractive capital city.
C Canberra is a lively modern attractive capital city.

Rewrite each sentence correctly.

17 'Will you visit Canberra while youre here!'

18 The national portrait gallery has some interesting paintings.

Reading and Comprehension

My review of *Circle*

Circle by Jeannie Baker is a picture book I love reading over and over. It is about birds called Bar-tailed Godwits. They are famous for flying a very long way without stopping. In winter they fly south from Alaska in the Arctic north to Australia and New Zealand. Then after feeding and resting they fly back again—making a circle of flight.

Each illustration is a collage. The colours are beautiful and I keep wanting to touch things in the pictures such as the knitted blanket on the bed, the wavy grass where the fox hunts and the soft fluffy chicks.

Another reason I love this book is because it shows you what happens in the real world—the circle of life. You see how the way we treat our own environment affects the lives of other living things. It makes you care about the world.

By Seb

1. The book, *Circle*, is about
   - **A** Alaska.
   - **B** Australia.
   - **C** Bar-tailed Godwits.
   - **D** Jeannie Baker.

2. Who wrote the review?
   - **A** Jeannie Baker
   - **B** Seb
   - **C** a Bar-tailed Godwit
   - **D** a fox

3. The illustrations are
   - **A** photographs.
   - **B** paintings.
   - **C** sketches.
   - **D** collages.

4. Why would the birds fly away from Alaska?
   - **A** The Arctic winter is too cold for them.
   - **B** They like to have a holiday.
   - **C** They have relatives in the south.
   - **D** It heats up in the summer.

5. What kind of birds are Bar-tailed Godwits?
   - **A** small songbirds
   - **B** talking parrots
   - **C** migrating water birds
   - **D** flightless birds

6. What makes the reviewer read the book 'over and over'?
   - **A** He is a birdwatcher.
   - **B** The book means a lot to him in different ways.
   - **C** He likes the pictures.
   - **D** He is a good reader.

Spelling

Rewrite the misspelt words.

1 The title of the book is <u>*Curcle*</u>.

2 Jeannie Baker is a <u>famus</u> Australian author.

3 I felt like touching the <u>nitted</u> blanket.

4 We need to take good care of our <u>envirenment</u>.

5 Write three words that rhyme with **eep**.

Vocabulary

Circle the word that has the nearest meaning to the underlined word.

6 She is a <u>famous</u> writer.

- **A** unknown
- **B** invisible
- **C** nameless
- **D** well-known

7 I'd like to <u>touch</u> the soft fur of the chicks.

- **A** feel
- **B** smell
- **C** pat
- **D** squeeze

8 Add a word from the text to the sentence.

How we treat our __________ has an effect on other living things.

9 Write a word from the text to match the meaning.

not being active __________

Circle the word on each line that does **not** belong.

10 shows hides reveals displays

11 sharp fluffy feathery soft

Grammar

12 Complete the sentence with a common noun from the text.

The colours of the __________ are beautiful.

13 Complete the sentence with an action (being) verb from the text.

These birds __________ from the north to the south.

14 Write a prepositional phrase from the text to tell **where**.

The book shows you what happens __________.

15 Choose a pronoun from the box to complete the sentence correctly.

he	she	it	you	they	I	we

Mary read the book *Circle* and __________ really liked it.

Punctuation

16 Circle the sentence that is punctuated correctly.

- **A** This book is interesting well illustrated, and clever.
- **B** This book is interesting, well illustrated and clever.
- **C** This book is interesting well illustrated and clever.

Rewrite each sentence correctly.

17 the Godwits flew 7145 km without stopping

18 Have you read *Circle* by Jeannie Baker.

Reading and Comprehension

Stop the digging!

Newsflash: Sydney

Workers are digging with their digging machines deep into the earth near the city of Sydney. They are getting the ground ready to build a new light rail track. It is thought this will help overcome Sydney's public transport crisis.

Some people say the digging MUST stop now. Already, the machines have dug up around 20 000 artefacts, objects made by humans in the past. They include Aboriginal spearheads, knife blades and marriage stones. The number of artefacts suggests the area may have been an important ceremonial meeting place.

It is believed there could be 50 000 or more artefacts still in the ground. If the digging continues these will be damaged, destroyed or lost. This means important information about our past could disappear.

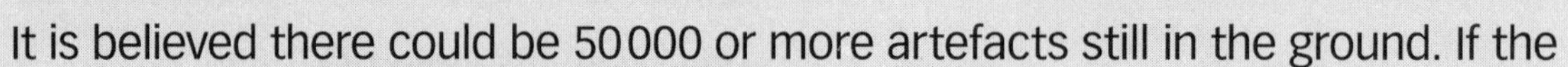

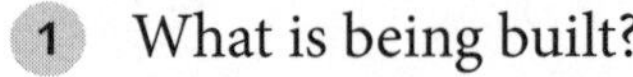

1. What is being built?
   - **A** a digging machine
   - **B** a light rail track
   - **C** a train
   - **D** objects

2. What are workers using to dig?
   - **A** earth
   - **B** spearheads
   - **C** digging machines
   - **D** knife blades

3. When do people say the digging must stop?
   - **A** now
   - **B** then
   - **C** soon
   - **D** later

4. Why do some think the digging should stop?
   - **A** 20 000 objects have already been dug up.
   - **B** The machines will damage or destroy important artefacts.
   - **C** Sydney doesn't need light rail.
   - **D** There is nothing new to learn about the past.

5. Which of these will the artefacts **not** tell us about?
   - **A** way of life
   - **B** culture
   - **C** light rail system
   - **D** beliefs

6. Who is most likely to want the digging to continue?
   - **A** the author of the newspaper article
   - **B** the Aboriginal people
   - **C** the light rail owners
   - **D** people who study the past

Spelling

Rewrite the misspelt words.

1 Light ralc is a form of transport.

2 The diggers found lots of objects in the erth.

3 The diging needs to stop.

4 The mashines are large and powerful.

5 Write three words that rhyme with **ast**.

Vocabulary

6 Circle the word that has the nearest meaning to the underlined word.
Thousands of artefacts were dug up.

A objects **B** spears
C knives **D** machines

7 Circle the word that has the nearest meaning to the underlined word.
I don't think we can overcome this problem.

A help **B** solve
C create **D** make

8 Add a word from the text to the sentence.
Sydney's public transport system is in ________.

9 Write a word from the text to match the meaning.
knowledge about someone or something

Circle the word on each line that does **not** belong.

10 heavy dense light weighty

11 damaged ruined preserved destroyed

Grammar

12 Complete the sentence with a common noun.
Light rail runs on a ________.

13 Complete the sentence with an action (being) verb from the text.
What do you plan to ________ on the ground where you are digging?

14 Write a prepositional phrase from the text to tell **where**.
Digging machines are now being used ________.

15 Choose a pronoun from the box to complete the sentence correctly.

he	she	it	you	they	I	we

Many objects were found and ________ were all made by humans.

Punctuation

16 Circle the sentence that is punctuated correctly.

A Is light rail similar to a tram?
B Is light rail similar to a tram.
C Is light rail similar to a tram!

Rewrite each sentence correctly.

17 the digging machines are very powerful

18 'stop digging at once'

Reading and Comprehension

Write a noun from the box in each space.

legs	playground	antennae	glasses	bodies	insects

1 Ms Wood: Get your magnifying ______________________, please. We are going outside into the ______________________ to study ______________________.

2 Jimmy: How do you know something is an insect?
Ms Wood: You can recognise insects by looking closely at their ______________________.

3 They have six ______________________, three body parts (head, thorax and abdomen) and two ______________________ on their heads.

Write a verb from the box in each space.

argued	built	fly	are digging	disagreed	care	stop

4 Some birds ______________________ all the way from Alaska to Australia. They do not ______________________ on the way.

5 It's important to ______________________ for our environment.

6 A new light rail track is being ______________________ at the moment. Workers ____________ ______________________ deep into the earth.

7 People ______________________ about where Canberra should be. They also ______________________ about what it should be called.

Spelling

The spelling mistakes in these sentences have been circled. Write the correct spelling on the lines.

8 No-one wants to be (crewel) to animals. ______________________

9 You should (heet) the eggs gently. ______________________

10 That's a really good (qestion)! ______________________

11 Australia became a (nashion) in 1901. ______________________

12 Canberra is our (capitol) city. ______________________

13 The birds fly in a huge (cercle). ______________________

14 They used digging (mashines). ______________________

15 They (fowned) lots of objects when they were digging. ______________________

Vocabulary

16 Circle the correct word in the brackets.
Insects each have a (pear / pair) of antennae.

17 Circle the word that means the opposite of **ends**.
finishes completes begins concludes

18 Circle the word that is similar in meaning to **afraid**.
brave calm confident frightened

Grammar

19 Add a common noun to the sentence.
You must crack ______________________ into a bowl to make an omelette.

20 Add a verb to the sentence.
I want to ______________________ the cello when I grow up.

21 Add a prepositional phrase to tell **where**.
The swan could see its reflection ______________________.

22 Add a pronoun to the sentence.
Pour out the milk and whisk ______________________ with the eggs.

Punctuation

Rewrite each sentence correctly.

23 'It looks like a spear' he said.

____

____

24 The birds were hungry thirsty and tired.

____

____

25 'stop that right now'

____

____

NAPLAN-STYLE 1 READING TEST

Reading

Life on the road

Dear Timmy and Sal

Your Nonny and I are having an amazing time. We love our new four-wheel drive and caravan. We're having plenty of adventures on the road. We've been to Canberra, where we dropped in on the Prime Minister, of course!

Now we are driving along the Eyre Highway through the Nullarbor Plain in southern Australia. If you're doing Latin at your school you'd know the name comes from the Latin words *nullus* meaning 'not any' and *arbor* meaning 'tree'—no trees. It is the longest straight stretch of road in the world.

You can see from the picture that we have to watch for animals on the road—camels, wombats and kangaroos. I wasn't expecting camels but we learned that around 100 000 wild camels were abandoned here after their use in building railroads. We've seen mobs of kangaroos beside the road.

See you at Christmas!

Love
Grandpa and Nonny

1. Where are Nonny and Grandpa?
   - **A** in Canberra
   - **B** on the Eyre Highway
   - **C** with the Prime Minister
   - **D** on the way home

2. What does **arbor** mean in Latin?
   - **A** not any
   - **B** tree
   - **C** no
   - **D** trees

3. The Nullarbor Plain is in
   - **A** southern Australia.
   - **B** South Australia.
   - **C** Western Australia.
   - **D** Eyre.

4. Timmy and Sal are Grandpa's
   - **A** children.
   - **B** parents.
   - **C** grandchildren.
   - **D** friends.

5. Grandpa wasn't expecting to see camels because
   - **A** he'd never seen a camel.
   - **B** they are not native animals.
   - **C** he thought they'd be helping build rail tracks elsewhere.
   - **D** his eyesight was not what it used to be.

6. Grandpa's postcard is
   - **A** cheerful and friendly.
   - **B** formal and proper.
   - **C** funny and unusual.
   - **D** anxious and upsetting.

Spelling

The spelling mistakes in these sentences have been underlined.
Write the correct spelling on the lines.

1. We saw the Prime Minister in Canbera. ____________________
2. We hooked the caravan to our fore-wheel drive. ____________________
3. It's a long straight stretch of rode. ____________________
4. They used the cammels to help build the railway. ____________________

Vocabulary

5. Which word is closest in meaning to **thinking it likely**?
   A inferring B expecting C imagining D judging
6. Which word does **not** belong?
   A small B long C tiny D little
7. Which word does **not** belong?
   A abandoned B left C deserted D found

Grammar

8. Which common noun names the animal Grandpa saw a mob of by the roadside?
   A lizards B camels C wombats D kangaroos
9. Which verb completes the sentence correctly?
   Grandpa and Nonny must ____________________ the road carefully in case animals are about.
   A speed B see C watch D notice
10. Which words tell **where** Grandpa and Nonny are having plenty of adventures?
    A at Canberra B on the road C on the Eyre Highway D with the camels

Punctuation

11. Which sentence is punctuated correctly?
    A We hope to see you when were back home.
    B We hope to see you when were back home
    C We hope to see you when we're back home.
    D We hope to see you when we're back home!
12. Which sentence is punctuated correctly?
    A 'You said you're doing Latin this term, didn't you?'
    B 'I think youre doing Latin at school, aren't you!'
    C 'have you ever studied Latin?'
    D 'Im going to study Latin next year.'

Reading and Comprehension

Things I like to do

I like:

- walking our dog, Rusty. I have to hold her lead tightly. Usually my little brother, George, comes with me but I won't let him hold the lead yet.
- cooking pancakes. I can even flip them over now. It's the only thing I can cook.
- staying at Gran and Pa's in the holidays. They let me collect eggs from their hens. I wear my gumboots when I'm there and splash about in the puddles near their barn. I saw a newborn lamb last time.
- reading funny joke and riddle books.
- playing soccer with my friends. Each week the coach chooses a man of the match. I've never been chosen but my friend Noah has been chosen twice.
- going ice skating at the weekend. I now can skate all the way around the rink without falling.

By Liam

1. What is the dog's name?
   - A George
   - B Liam
   - C Rusty
   - D Sonny

2. Where does Liam wear gumboots?
   - A at his gran and pa's
   - B at ice skating
   - C at soccer
   - D at home

3. What sort of books does Liam like reading?
   - A soccer
   - B riddle
   - C cooking
   - D animal

4. Why doesn't Liam let George hold the lead?
   - A Liam doesn't like his brother.
   - B George is not strong enough yet.
   - C Liam wants his dog all to himself.
   - D Liam wants to show who is boss.

5. Where do Liam's grandparents live?
   - A in a unit in a high-rise building
   - B in a retirement home
   - C in a house in the inner city
   - D in a house in the country

6. Is Liam a boastful boy?
   - A Yes. He boasts about what a good ice skater he is.
   - B Yes. He thinks he is going to be man of the match at soccer.
   - C No. He says what he can do well but also what he can't do.
   - D No. He is just shy.

Spelling

Rewrite the misspelt words.

1 I hold Rusty's lead titely so she can't run off.

2 Gran and Pa have lams and cows at their place.

3 My frend is coming to stay over this weekend.

4 I like colecting the eggs for our breakfast.

5 Write three words that end with the letters **old**.

Vocabulary

Circle the word that has the nearest meaning to the underlined word.

6 Mum won't allow me to use her computer.

A forbid B let
C encourage D promise

7 Dad taught me how to flip the pancakes over.

A send B throw
C plunge D flick

8 Add a word from the text to the sentence.

My brother likes to ______ stamps and keep them in an album.

9 Write a word from the text to match the meaning.

most of the time ______

Circle the word on each line that does **not** belong.

10 boring funny humorous amusing

11 sole only several single

Grammar

12 Complete the sentence with a proper noun from the text.

My brother, ______, is three years younger than I am.

13 Complete the sentence with a sensing verb from the text.

I ______ some new-born lambs yesterday.

14 Write a prepositional phrase from the text to tell **when**.

It's fun staying at Gran's ______.

15 Choose a pronoun from the box to complete the sentence correctly.

he	she	it	you	they	I	we

Noah said ______ put his trophy on his bookshelf.

Punctuation

16 Circle the sentence that is punctuated correctly.

A Its fun skating around the ice rink!
B It's fun skating around the ice rink.
C Its fun skating around the ice rink.

Rewrite each sentence correctly.

17 'Do you like reading joke books.'

18 The sports I like are, ice skating and soccer!

Reading and Comprehension

UNIT 9A

Antarctic krill

Living in the Southern Ocean which surrounds Antarctica, a continent of glaciers and ice sheets, krill play a vital part in the food chain. Female krill lay up to 8000 eggs at a time and it is estimated Antarctic krill probably have the largest population of any species on earth.

Antarctic krill grow to about 6 cm in length. They have large black eyes and semitransparent shells. They feed on minute organisms in the ocean and eat algae from the underside of sea ice. Krill often move together in giant swarms that stretch for kilometres in all directions. This gives them some protection.

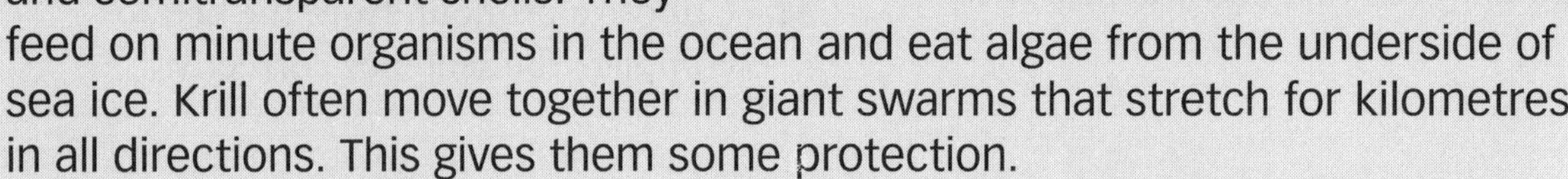

Whales, seals, penguins, fish and birds eat around half of the krill population every year. Blue whales, for example, eat up to 40 million krill daily. In recent times the number of krill has declined. Many scientists are saying it is important to introduce ways to protect their numbers.

1. What is Antarctica?
   - **A** a glacier
   - **B** an ice sheet
   - **C** an ocean
   - **D** a continent

2. What size are the plants and animals eaten by krill?
   - **A** large
   - **B** middle-sized
   - **C** minute
   - **D** tiny

3. Where do the Antarctic krill live?
   - **A** in the air
   - **B** in the waters around Antarctica
   - **C** in the rivers
   - **D** in the sea

4. Why might you see a krill's digestive tract?
   - **A** It is very large.
   - **B** Its shell is semitransparent.
   - **C** It is brightly coloured.
   - **D** It is shiny.

5. Why do krill float in giant swarms?
   - **A** to make swimming easier
   - **B** The tides blow them together.
   - **C** to keep warm
   - **D** for safety reasons

6. Why is protecting krill important?

   ....

   ....

   ....

Spelling

Rewrite the misspelt words.

1 Krill are part of the food chane.

2 My little finger is about the lenth of a krill.

3 Blue wails eat masses of krill.

4 Winter is a very cold seeson in Antarctica.

5 Write three words that end with the letters **eed**.

Vocabulary

Circle the word that has the nearest meaning to the underlined word.

6 Krill move in large swarms.
A patterns B designs
C groups D baskets

7 Antarctic krill are a species of krill.
A kind B specialty
C relative D friend

8 Add a word from the text to the sentence.
The krill population has ______ recently.

9 Write a word from the text to match the meaning.
being kept safe from attack ______

Circle the word on each line that does **not** belong.

10 expanded declined increased grown

11 vital unimportant significant essential

Grammar

12 Complete the sentence with a proper noun from the text.
The ocean that surrounds ______ is full of plants and animals.

13 Complete the sentence with a relating (having) verb from the text.
Krill ______ a very large population.

14 Write a prepositional phrase from the text to tell **when**.
Blue whales eat millions of krill
______.

15 Choose a pronoun from the box to complete the sentence correctly.

he	she	it	you	they	I	we

Mum and Dad say ______ want to visit Antarctica.

Punctuation

16 Circle the sentence that is punctuated correctly.
A Whales, seals, and penguins depend on krill!
B Whales, seals and penguins depend on krill!
C Whales, seals and penguins depend on krill.

Rewrite each sentence correctly.

17 Therell be problems if krill numbers arent protected.

18 It's shell can be seen through

UNIT 10A

Reading and Comprehension

Things I don't like to do

I don't like:

- eating my green vegetables every night. I groan when I see them taking up so much space on my plate.
- coming last in the marathon at school. I must get fitter!
- having so much homework that I don't feel like sitting at my desk.
- being sent to my room. It is slightly better than losing my pocket money but not much.
- going on long car journeys in the holidays when I have to share the back seat with my sisters, Rosie and Belle. They are as enormous as giants.
- getting new school shoes. They always squeak or give me blisters.
- sitting behind a tall person who is wearing a hat when we go to the movies. Mum tells me to use a booster seat but I feel too embarrassed.

By Bec

1. What kind of vegetables does Bec not like?
   - **A** cooked
   - **B** raw
   - **C** green
   - **D** large

2. What sort of car journeys does Bec dislike?
   - **A** any
   - **B** long
   - **C** short
   - **D** medium

3. What new things does Bec dislike getting?
   - **A** pocket money
   - **B** booster seats
   - **C** hats
   - **D** shoes

4. Is Bec a sporty type of girl?
   - **A** probably not
   - **B** definitely
   - **C** certainly
   - **D** clearly

5. Why does Bec say her sisters are as enormous as giants?
   - **A** They take up so much of her space in the car.
   - **B** She dislikes them.
   - **C** They remind her of fairy tales.
   - **D** They are larger than everyone else's sisters.

6. Bec's parents can be described as
   - **A** mean.
   - **B** thoughtless.
   - **C** caring.
   - **D** unkind.

Spelling

Rewrite the misspelt words.

1 I like <u>vedgetables</u> much more than I used to.

2 I hate <u>loosing</u> my pocket money as a punishment.

3 Last holidays we went on a <u>jurney</u> to another state.

4 It makes me feel <u>embarased</u>.

5 Write three words that end with the letters **eat**.

Vocabulary

Circle the word that has the nearest meaning to the underlined word.

6 He had <u>enormous</u> feet for his age.

- **A** mountainous
- **B** gigantic
- **C** large
- **D** massive

7 I am <u>slightly</u> taller than you are.

- **A** barely
- **B** mostly
- **C** almost
- **D** completely

8 Add a word from the text to the sentence.

I go red in the face when I feel ______.

9 Write a word from the text to match the meaning.

use something with others ______

Circle the word on each line that does **not** belong.

10 moan sigh cheer whimper

11 old new worn-out threadbare

Grammar

12 Complete the sentence with a proper noun from the text.

Rosie takes up even more room than ______.

13 Complete the sentence with a sensing verb from the text.

I ______ cross when I get too much homework.

14 Write a prepositional phrase from the text to tell **when**.

We go on long journeys ______.

15 Choose a pronoun from the box to complete the sentence correctly.

he	she	it	you	they	I	we

I have new shoes so I know ______ will have blisters by tonight.

Punctuation

16 Circle the sentence that is punctuated correctly.

- **A** I have new shoes, and a new hat.
- **B** I have new shoes and a new hat!
- **C** I have new shoes and a new hat.

Rewrite each sentence correctly.

17 I dont like having a strict bedtime

18 Are there things you don't like too!

Reading and Comprehension

How our states and territories got their names

The names of Australia's states and territories mainly came from their names as separate British colonies. New South Wales was the name Captain Cook, the British explorer, gave to this 'new' south land when he claimed it for his country. He named it after Wales in England. No-one is quite sure why.

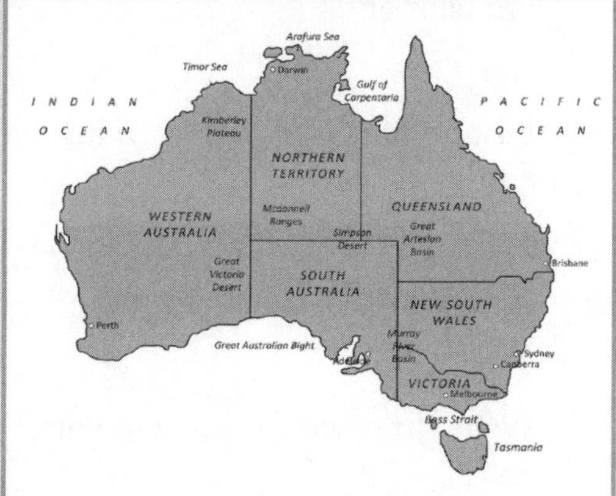

In the 1850s, the colonies of Victoria and Queensland separated from New South Wales and took names that honoured Queen Victoria. At the time, she was a popular, well-loved queen of England.

The names for South Australia, Western Australia and the Northern Territory refer loosely to their location on the map. The Australian Capital Territory houses Australia's capital, Canberra.

The Dutch explorer Abel Tasman discovered the island of Tasmania in 1642. He named it Van Dieman's Land after a sponsor. The name reminded people that the colony began as a convict settlement and in 1856 it was renamed Tasmania.

1. Who gave New South Wales its name?
   - **A** Captain Cook
   - **B** Abel Tasman
   - **C** Queen Victoria
   - **D** Van Dieman

2. Which state has the name of a queen?
   - **A** Queensland
   - **B** New South Wales
   - **C** South Australia
   - **D** Victoria

3. Who discovered Tasmania?
   - **A** Captain Cook
   - **B** Abel Tasman
   - **C** Queen Victoria
   - **D** Van Dieman

4. What do the inverted commas around **new** on line 4 suggest?
   - **A** that the word is spoken
   - **B** that the land was very new
   - **C** that the land was not really new at all
   - **D** that the land was like Wales

5. How did the Tasmanian people feel about their convict origins before 1856?
   - **A** embarrassed
   - **B** proud
   - **C** satisfied
   - **D** pleased

6. The name choices for Australia's states and territories are mainly
   - **A** imaginative and weird.
   - **B** sensible and practical.
   - **C** unusual and odd.
   - **D** romantic and dreamy.

Spelling

Rewrite the misspelt words.

1 Austraylia became a nation in 1901.

2 Queen Victoria was quite a poppular queen.

3 Canbera is a capital city.

4 Tasman disscovered Tasmania in 1642.

5 Write three words that end with the letters **ave**.

Vocabulary

Circle the word that has the nearest meaning to the underlined word.

6 Some areas separated from New South Wales in the 1850s.

A united B parted
C joined D married

7 Australia began as a convict settlement

A ended B ceased
C started D finished

8 Add a word from the text to the sentence.

Captain James Cook was a British ______.

9 Write a word from the text to match the meaning.

given a new name ______

Circle the word on each line that does **not** belong.

10 popular, well-loved, disliked, admired

11 loosely, roughly, exactly, nearly

Grammar

12 Complete the sentence with a proper noun from the text.

______ is in England.

13 Complete the sentence with a relating (being) verb from the text.

New South Wales ______ named by Captain Cook.

14 Write a prepositional phrase from the text to tell **when**.

Victoria separated from New South Wales ______.

15 Choose a pronoun from the box to complete the sentence correctly.

he	she	it	you	they	I	we

Perth is the capital of Western Australia and ______ is known for its wildflowers.

Punctuation

16 Circle the sentence that is punctuated correctly.

A Abel Tasman, the Dutch explorer, discovered Tasmania in 1642.

B Abel Tasman the Dutch explorer discovered Tasmania in 1642!

C Abel Tasman the Dutch explorer discovered Tasmania in 1642.

Rewrite each sentence correctly.

17 Western Australia, is the largest of Australias states.

18 Queen Victoria ruled England, for many years.

Reading and Comprehension

The Olympic Games

Long ago in Olympia in Ancient Greece, sporting and religious festivals were held every four years. Male athletes from around 100 city states competed with each other. Events included running, discus- and javelin-throwing, wrestling and chariot racing.

The first modern Olympic Games was held in Athens in 1896. Male athletes from thirteen countries took part. It was at this Olympics that the first marathon race was held.

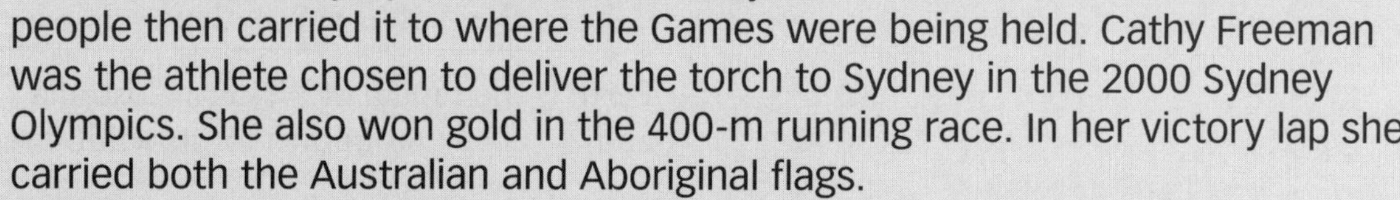

In 1936 another tradition began. The Olympic flame was lit in Olympia in Greece. A relay of people then carried it to where the Games were being held. Cathy Freeman was the athlete chosen to deliver the torch to Sydney in the 2000 Sydney Olympics. She also won gold in the 400-m running race. In her victory lap she carried both the Australian and Aboriginal flags.

At present, the Olympic Games is a four-yearly international sporting competition in which athletes from over 200 nations compete.

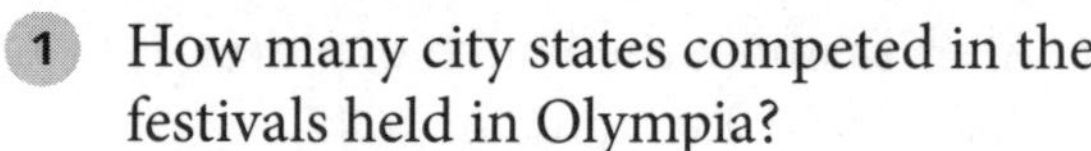

1. How many city states competed in the festivals held in Olympia?
   - **A** well over 100
   - **B** exactly thirteen
   - **C** more than 200
   - **D** around 100

2. In which city was the first modern Olympic Games held?
   - **A** Olympia
   - **B** Athens
   - **C** Marathon
   - **D** Sydney

3. Where is the Olympic flame lit before each Olympic Games?
   - **A** Athens
   - **B** Sydney
   - **C** Olympia
   - **D** Marathon

4. How are the modern Olympics different from the older ones?
   - **A** Females are allowed to compete.
   - **B** They occur every four years.
   - **C** They are religious.
   - **D** They don't have a marathon.

5. What is the Olympic flame carried in?
   - **A** a relay baton
   - **B** a flag
   - **C** a torch
   - **D** a javelin

6. Why do people think the Olympics Games are important events?

Spelling

Rewrite the misspelt words.

1 In 2016 the Olimpic Games were held in Rio.

2 Many different peeple are asked to carry the torch.

3 Only mails took part in the Greek festivals.

4 You can win a goaled medal at the Games.

5 Write three words that end with the letters **ate**.

Vocabulary

Circle the word that has the nearest meaning to the underlined word.

6 Cathy Freeman ran a victory lap.
- A gold
- B losing
- C winning
- D relay

7 You have to run a long distance in a marathon.
- A way
- B space
- C size
- D road

8 Add a word from the text to the sentence.
She carried an Australian flag and an ______ flag.

9 Write a word from the text to match the meaning.
between nations ______

Circle the word on each line that does **not** belong.

10 ancient, new, old, aged

11 deliver, take, carry, keep

Grammar

12 Complete the sentence with a proper noun from the text.
In 2000 the Olympics were held in ______.

13 Complete the sentence with a relating (being) verb from the text.
It ______ in 1896 that the first marathon was run.

14 Write a prepositional phrase from the text to tell **when**.
Over 200 nations compete in the Olympics ______.

15 Choose a pronoun from the box to complete the sentence correctly.

he	she	it	you	they	I	we

Have ______ ever run a marathon, Mum?

Punctuation

16 Circle the sentence that is punctuated correctly.
- A Events now include, the high jump long jump and pole vault.
- B Events now include the high jump, long jump and pole vault.
- C Events now include the high jump long jump, and pole vault.

Rewrite each sentence correctly.

17 Female athletes couldnt compete in the past.

18 Have you ever been to the Olympics, Mary I asked

Reading and Comprehension

UNIT 13A

Bastille Day

Back Compose Reply Reply all Forward Delete Move Print Mark More

To: Peter@biglake.com
Hello there, big cousin

I have to give a talk in class next week about Bastille Day. I know it is celebrated on 14 July in France and that you don't have to go to school on that day! Can you tell me what the French are celebrating, please?

Au revoir (for now)
Lily

> To: Lily@littlecove.com.au
> Hi Lily
> I see your French is improving! J
>
> Bastille Day celebrates the day the people stormed a famous prison, the Bastille, and set its prisoners free. It happened in 1789 when many French people were angry with the way the king and queen ruled them. They ignored the poor and starving and kept enjoying their banquets and riches. When people complained they were thrown into prison.
>
> I think Bastille Day is a way of remembering the brave people who fought for freedom and justice.
>
> Hope that helps, little cuz!
> Peter

1 When does Lily have to give her talk?
- **A** 14 July
- **B** 1789
- **C** next week
- **D** Bastille Day

2 Who ruled France before 1789?
- **A** a king
- **B** a queen
- **C** the people
- **D** a king and queen

3 How are Lily and Peter related?
- **A** as brother and sister
- **B** as cousins
- **C** They're not.
- **D** as aunt and uncle

4 'I see your French is improving! ☺' is
- **A** praise for Lily.
- **B** Peter's joke.
- **C** a cross remark.
- **D** a well-known saying.

5 People wanted the prisoners released in 1789 because
- **A** they were put there unfairly.
- **B** they'd been there long enough.
- **C** the prisons needed to be cleaned.
- **D** the prisons were overcrowded.

6 What is Peter's attitude to Lily?
- **A** stern
- **B** disapproving
- **C** friendly
- **D** prickly

Spelling

Rewrite the misspelt words.

1 Bastille Day is <u>selebrated</u> on 14 July.

______

2 The king and <u>qeen</u> were taken from the throne.

______

3 The poor people felt angry about the <u>banqets</u> of the rich.

______

4 Many people have <u>fort</u> for freedom in the past.

______

5 Write three words that end with the letters **ought**.

______

______

______

Vocabulary

Circle the word that has the nearest meaning to the underlined word.

6 The Bastille was <u>stormed</u> in France in 1789.

A rained on B attacked
C viewed D celebrated

7 There were plenty of <u>complaints</u> about their cruelty.

A tears B compliments
C roars D protests

8 Add a word from the text to the sentence.

Bastille Day is sometimes ______ with fireworks.

9 Write a word from the text to match the meaning.

getting better ______

Circle the word on each line that does **not** belong.

10 rich wealthy penniless well-to-do

11 cross furious calm angry

Grammar

12 Complete the sentence with a proper noun from the text.

______ replied to Lily's email.

13 Complete the sentence with a saying verb from the text.

The king and queen threw people in prison when they ______.

14 Write a prepositional phrase from the text to tell **when**.

Bastille Day is celebrated ______.

15 Choose a pronoun from the box to complete the sentence correctly.

he	she	it	you	they	I	we

The King and Queen threw people in prison when they ______.

Punctuation

16 Circle the sentence that is punctuated correctly.

A Its a French celebration.
B It's a french celebration.
C It's a French celebration.

Rewrite each sentence correctly.

17 'How do they celebrate bastille day in France.'

______

______

______

18 The celebrations were held in paris!

______

______

______

Reading and Comprehension

The greedy dog

One day a dog was looking through the window of a butcher's shop. He noticed an enormous, juicy bone on the counter. The dog didn't waste a minute. He plunged through the curtain of plastic strips. Then he ran off with the bone clamped firmly between his teeth.

Trotting proudly through the village of Pridedale, the dog hoped everyone was admiring how clever he was. As he crossed the bridge to his home near the caravan park, he glanced down at the water. There to his surprise he saw another dog with an even bigger bone. He wanted it. He had to have it immediately!

He flung himself into the water, jaws snapping wildly. At nothing! Dog and bone had disappeared. And the bone he'd stolen was now lost too. Cold, wet, hungry and just a little bit ashamed, the greedy dog crept home.

Adapted from an Aesop's fable

1 Where was the bone in the shop?
- A in the window
- B in the doorway
- C on the counter
- D behind the plastic strips

2 Where did the dog live?
- A in a butcher's shop
- B under the bridge
- C beside the river
- D near the caravan park

3 How did the dog trot through the village?
- A quickly
- B slowly
- C proudly
- D immediately

4 How did the dog in the water disappear?
- A It swam away very quickly.
- B It was only a reflection in the water.
- C It hid under the bridge.
- D It dived under the water.

5 How did the stolen bone get lost?
- A The dog dropped it into the river when he dived in.
- B The butcher got it back.
- C The dog dropped it when he got out of the river.
- D It was stolen from the dog.

6 What is the moral of this story?
- A If you look for harm you'll find it.
- B Be grateful for what you have.
- C Don't put things off.
- D Slow and steady wins the race.

Spelling

Rewrite the misspelt words.

1. The dog didn't waist any time at all.

2. He hopped he could have an even bigger bone.

3. Did you see its face reflected in the warter?

4. The dog was greedy and foolish to.

5. Write three words that end with the letters **one**.

Vocabulary

Circle the word that has the nearest meaning to the underlined word.

6. Did you see how he clamped the bone between his teeth?
   - A crunched
   - B chewed
   - C gripped
   - D put

7. To his surprise he saw an even bigger bone!
   - A astonishment
   - B curiosity
   - C disappointment
   - D happiness

8. Add a word from the text to the sentence.
   The dog felt guilty and a bit ______ of his behaviour.

9. Write a word from the text to match the meaning.
   not anything ______

Circle the word on each line that does **not** belong.

10. vanish, disappear, appear, dissolve

11. glance, peek, stare, peep

Grammar

12. Complete the sentence with a proper noun from the text.
    Have you visited the village of ______?

13. Complete the sentence with a sensing verb from the text.
    At first he trotted proudly but later he ______ home.

14. Write a prepositional phrase from the text to tell **when**.
    The greedy dog ______ down at its reflection.

15. Choose a pronoun from the box to complete the sentence correctly.

he	she	it	you	they	I	we

The butcher and I saw the dog steal the bone and ______ felt very cross.

Punctuation

16. Circle the sentence that is punctuated correctly.
    - A The dog had the bone in its mouth.
    - B The dog had the bone in it's mouth.
    - C The Dog had the bone in its mouth.

Rewrite each sentence correctly.

17. Nothing would ever stop him.

18. Warm, cosy dry and happy he snuggled in front of the fire.

Reading and Comprehension

Helping our planet

Ms Knight: How do you help the planet at your place?

Charlie: We recycle everything. The other day we got a WELL DONE sticker on our bin from the council!

Sophie: My mum organises car pools each week to share driving to school sports and other activities.

Akito: I showed my parents a picture of sea creatures who died because their stomachs were full of plastic bags. We don't bring plastic bags home from Friskos any more. We use canvas bags to carry our shopping.

Ms Knight: That's all good news. I've just heard about another way to save the planet from more landfill. Some of the big supermarkets provide red bins where you can put the plastic packaging you would normally throw away—things like bubble wrap, ice-cream wrappers and cereal box liners. It will be recycled and turned into park benches and play equipment. Good idea?

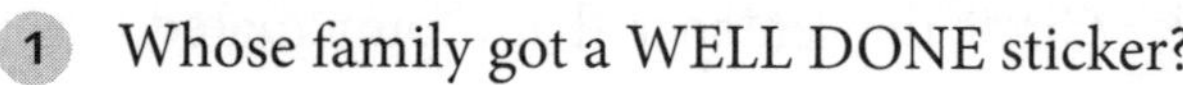

1. Whose family got a WELL DONE sticker?
   - **A** Ms Knight's
   - **B** Charlie's
   - **C** Sophie's
   - **D** Akito's

2. Whose mum organises a car pool?
   - **A** Ms Knight's
   - **B** Charlie's
   - **C** Sophie's
   - **D** Akito's

3. What was found in the stomachs of the sea creatures who died?
   - **A** plastic bags
   - **B** ice-cream wrappers
   - **C** bubble wrap
   - **D** canvas

4. Why does Akito's family use canvas bags for their shopping?
   - **A** to use more canvas
   - **B** to use less plastic
   - **C** to please the supermarkets
   - **D** to add to the landfill

5. How would car pools help the planet?
   - **A** reduce landfill
   - **B** help overcrowding
   - **C** reduce pollution
   - **D** saves animal's lives

6. What kind of teacher is Ms Knight?
   - **A** strict
   - **B** unkind
   - **C** thoughtless
   - **D** thoughtful

Spelling

Rewrite the misspelt words.

1 We have brightly coloured recicling bins at our school.

....

2 That whale dyed from eating plastic.

....

3 Bubble rap can be put in the new red bins.

....

4 Do you take shoping bags with you to the supermarket?

....

5 Write three words that end with the letters **ull**.

....

....

....

Vocabulary

Circle the word that has the nearest meaning to the underlined word.

6 The supermarkets provide the bins.

A show **B** contribute
C arrange **D** send

7 We normally put plastic wrap in our bin.

A always **B** sometimes
C occasionally **D** usually

8 Add a word from the text to the sentence.

Sea .... suffer from plastic in the ocean.

9 Write a word from the text to match the meaning.

makes arrangements for ....

Circle the word on each line that does **not** belong.

10 reply say speak hear

11 packed empty jammed full

Grammar

12 Complete the sentence with a proper noun from the text.

We take our canvas bags to .... when we shop.

13 Complete the sentence with a relating (being) verb from the text.

They died because their stomachs .... full of plastic bags.

14 Write a prepositional phrase from the text to tell **when**.

Mum emails a roster ....

15 Choose a pronoun from the box to complete the sentence correctly.

he	she	it	you	they	I	we

Do .... have a worm farm in your garden?

Punctuation

16 Circle the sentence that is punctuated correctly.

A We recycle bottles, paper and plastic.
B We recycle bottles paper, and plastic.
C We recycle bottles, paper and plastic!

Rewrite each sentence correctly.

17 That's a wonderful idea.

....

....

....

18 Youre helping to make a difference.

....

....

....

Reading and Comprehension

Write proper nouns from the box in each space.

Australia	Wales	Antarctica	Rusty	George	Abel Tasman

1 I take my dog, ____________________, for a walk each day. My brother, ____________________, likes to come with me.

2 The continent of ____________________ is a land of glaciers and ice sheets.

3 Captain Cook named New South Wales after ____________________. Tasmania was named after ____________________. Tasmania is off the mainland of ____________________.

Write a word from the box in each space.

Aboriginal	collect	gold	victory	story	celebration
puddles	eggs	Bastille Day	gumboots	grateful	

4 When I'm at Gran's I like to wear my ____________________ so I can kick the water in the ____________________. I also like to ____________________ the ____________________ from the hens.

5 Cathy Freeman carried the Australian and the ____________________ flags in her ____________________ lap after winning a ____________________ medal.

6 We had a ____________________ in our French class at school in honour of ____________________.

7 The moral of the ____________________ was be ____________________ for what you have.

Spelling

The spelling mistakes in these sentences have been circled. Write the correct spelling on the lines.

8 Hold on (titely) to Rusty's lead. ____________________

9 I hope you don't (loose) your rugby game. ____________________

10 Both (mails) and females take part in the Olympics now. ____________________

11 Please don't (weight) for me. ____________________

12 The king and (qeen) enjoyed their banquet. ____________________

13 They (fort) for freedom. ____________________

14 She left it (neer) the seat. ____________________

15 The fish (dyed) from swallowing too much plastic. ____________________

Answers

Unit 1A page 8

1. B. See lines 4–5.
2. C. See lines 10–11.
3. D. See lines 9–10.
4. A. You can work out her family is pleased about Rosie playing rugby because her dad helps her keep fit and they all go and watch her try out.
5. A. You can work out Rosie is nervous because there are so many others who also want to get into the district team. This makes it less likely she'll be selected.
6. C. You can judge Rosie is very keen to get into the district team because she is willing to try again if she fails.

Unit 1B page 9

1. team
2. brother
3. week
4. family
5. for example, ham, jam, ram, slam, tram
6. C.
7. A.
8. chosen
9. determined
10. high
11. likes
12. brothers
13. play
14. at the park
15. he
16. C.
17. Jem is good at rugby.
18. I'll be trying out next weekend.

Unit 2A page 10

1. D. See lines 2–3.
2. C. See line 5.
3. D. See line 11.
4. B. You can work out the other ducks made fun of him because he didn't look the same as they did.
5. B. You can work out he was so used to being treated unkindly that he thought the swans would treat him in the same unkind way.
6. C. You can judge the ducks were mainly responsible for his unhappiness because they made cruel fun of him and he was miserable for a long time after.

Unit 2B page 11

1. finally
2. cruel
3. treated
4. beaks
5. for example, bun, fun, gun, run, stun
6. C.
7. A.
8. shelter
9. ugly
10. easy
11. contented
12. ducklings
13. hid
14. in the stream
15. you
16. C.
17. The sad, frightened duck ran away from home.
18. 'You are so big and ugly,' she quacked.

Unit 3A page 12

1. C. See line 12.
2. A. See line 13.
3. B. See line 18.
4. C. You can work out the fillings given are examples for the cook to choose from.
5. D. You can work out that all of the ingredients need to be good for you for the meal to be described as healthy.
6. C. You can judge the language is mostly straightforward and practical, stating what is needed and what needs to be done to cook an omelette.

Unit 3B page 13

1. chopped
2. bowl
3. draw
4. heat
5. for example, bake, cake, lake, make, shake
6. C.
7. D.
8. herbs
9. mixture
10. ends
11. firmly
12. mushrooms/onions/tomatoes/ham/cheese
13. foam
14. into the bowl
15. they
16. B.
17. If the heat is too high, you'll burn the eggs.
18. It's easy to poach an egg.

Unit 4A page 14

1. C. See lines 2–3.
2. B. See lines 7–8.
3. A. See lines 11–12.
4. C. You can work out this is a conversation between a teacher and her class. They plan to go outside afterwards so you can infer they are in a classroom.
5. B. You can work out the children will use their magnifying glasses to enlarge the insects so they can see their parts more closely.
6. You can judge the children are very likely to find insects in the playground as there are so many of them everywhere.

Answers

Unit 4B page 15

1. insect
2. question
3. glasses
4. pair
5. for example, blink, ink, pink, think, shrink
6. D.
7. C.
8. estimate
9. antennae
10. outside
11. important
12. insect
13. do
14. on their heads
15. it
16. C.
17. Spiders aren't insects.
18. This bug has six legs, three body parts and two antennae.

Unit 5A page 16

1. B. See lines 2–4.
2. D. See lines 4–5.
3. C. See line 15.
4. A. You can work out the shortened words are Sydney, Melbourne, Adelaide, Perth, Brisbane and Hobart—the names of the capital cities in the six Australian states.
5. A and D. You can work out that there are women in parliament today and no-one believes any longer that you have to be cold to think well.
6. A. You judge that words such as 'strikingly modern' and 'significant' suggest the author is impressed with Canberra as a city.

Unit 5B page 17

1. nation
2. coast
3. Disagreement
4. capital
5. for example, blame, came, game, name, same
6. B.
7. C.
8. Australia
9. disagreement
10. useful
11. unfriendly
12. city
13. joined
14. on a lake
15. it
16. B.
17. 'Will you visit Canberra while you're here?'
18. The National Portrait Gallery has some interesting paintings.

Unit 6A page 18

1. C. See lines 3–4.
2. B. See line 19.
3. D. See line 11.
4. A. You can work out the birds won't survive the Arctic winter so they migrate south where it is warmer.
5. C. You can work out from the picture that Bar-tailed Godwits are water birds and you learn from the text that they migrate regularly.
6. B. You can judge there are several different things the reviewer loves about the book that draw him back to reading it repeatedly.

Unit 6B page 19

1. *Circle*
2. famous
3. knitted
4. environment
5. for example, beep, creep, deep, keep, peep, sweep
6. D.
7. A.
8. environment/world
9. resting
10. hides
11. sharp
12. illustrations
13. fly
14. in the real world
15. she
16. B.
17. The Godwits flew 7145 km without stopping!
18. Have you read *Circle* by Jeannie Baker?

Unit 7A page 20

1. B. See lines 5–6.
2. C. See lines 3–4.
3. A. See lines 8–9.
4. B. You can work out some want the digging to stop because they think the many objects that are still in the earth will be damaged or destroyed. This would stop us gathering important information from the site.
5. C. The light rail system didn't exist at the time the objects were made.
6. C. You can judge those with a strong interest in keeping the digging going are the light rail owners who may lose money if their work is stopped.

Answers

Unit 7B page 21

1. rail
2. earth
3. digging
4. machines
5. for example, blast, fast, last, mast, past
6. A.
7. B.
8. crisis
9. information
10. light
11. preserved
12. track
13. build
14. near the city of Sydney
15. they
16. A.
17. The digging machines are very powerful.
18. 'Stop digging at once!'

Revision 1 pages 22–23

1. glasses, playground, insects
2. bodies
3. legs, antennae
4. fly, stop
5. care
6. built, are digging
7. disagreed, argued
8. cruel
9. heat
10. question
11. nation
12. capital
13. circle
14. machines
15. found
16. pair
17. begins
18. frightened
19. eggs
20. play
21. in the stream/water/pond/ river
22. it
23. 'It looks like a spear,' he said.
24. The birds were hungry, thirsty and tired.
25. 'Stop that right now!'

NAPLAN-style Reading Test 1 page 24

1. B. See line 7.
2. B. See line 10.
3. A. See line 8.
4. C. You can work out Timmy and Sal are at school so they are children. This implies they are Grandpa's and Nonny's grandchildren.
5. B. You can work out the animals Grandpa expected to see were native animals (kangaroos and wombats). Camels are not native to Australia so he wasn't expecting to see them.
6. A. You can judge Grandpa passes on happy news about their travels and even makes a joke about visiting the Prime Minister. He writes to the children in a warm, affectionate way.

NAPLAN-style Conventions of Language Test 1 page 25

1. Canberra
2. four-wheel
3. road
4. camels
5. B.
6. B.
7. D.
8. D.
9. C.
10. B.
11. C.
12. A.

Unit 8A page 26

1. C. See line 3.
2. A. See lines 9–11.
3. B. See line 13.
4. B. You can work out Rusty, the dog, is big and strong and George is still small and not yet strong enough to hold the lead tightly.
5. D. You can work out they live in a house in the country because they have animals and a barn.
6. C. You can judge Liam is not boastful because he just states what he can do and doesn't exaggerate or show off about himself. He is also honest about what he can't do.

Unit 8B page 27

1. tightly
2. lambs
3. friend
4. collecting
5. for example, bold, cold, gold, hold, sold
6. B.
7. D.
8. collect
9. usually
10. boring
11. several
12. George
13. saw
14. in the holidays
15. he
16. B.
17. 'Do you like reading joke books?'
18. The sports I like are ice skating and soccer.

Unit 9A page 28

1. D. See line 3.
2. C. See lines 12–13.
3. B. See lines 2–4.
4. B. You can work out a semitransparent shell can be seen through. This means you could see the digestive tract inside.

5. D. You can work out floating together makes it harder for predators to eat them.
6. Answers may vary. You can judge if krill numbers continue to decline there are many animals who would be without food and unlikely to survive in the harsh Antarctic climate.

Unit 9B page 29

1. chain
2. length
3. whales
4. season
5. for example, deed, feed, greed, need, seed
6. C.
7. A.
8. declined
9. protection
10. declined
11. unimportant
12. Antarctica
13. have
14. daily
15. they
16. C.
17. There'll be problems if krill numbers aren't protected.
18. Its shell can be seen through.

Unit 10A page 30

1. C. See lines 2–3.
2. B. See line 12.
3. D. See line 14.
4. A. You can work out if Bec comes last in the marathon and admits she needs to get fitter she is probably not sporty.
5. A. You can work out Bec's sisters take up so much space on the back seat that she feels as if they are as big as giants. She is exaggerating.
6. C. You can judge Bec's parents care for her very well. They see she eats her greens so she'll be healthy, teach her to do the right thing and take her on holidays and outings.

Unit 10B page 31

1. vegetables
2. losing
3. journey
4. embarrassed
5. for example, beat, heat, meat, seat, treat
6. C.
7. A.
8. embarrassed
9. share
10. cheer
11. new
12. Belle
13. feel
14. in the holidays
15. I
16. C.
17. I don't like having a strict bedtime.
18. Are there things you don't like too?

Unit 11A page 32

1. A. See lines 3–4.
2. D. See lines 7–9.
3. B. See line 16.
4. C. You can work out that the inverted commas show it was not really new even though Captain Cook named it new. Aboriginal people had lived on this land for hundreds of thousands of years.
5. A. You can work out they wanted to forget about the colony starting off with convicts because they were embarrassed to be linked with people who had broken the law.
6. B. You can judge the names are mainly connected with people's names or their location on the map. This makes them practical and straightforward.

Unit 11B page 33

1. Australia
2. popular
3. Canberra
4. discovered
5. for example, cave, gave, have, wave, shave
6. B.
7. C.
8. explorer
9. renamed
10. disliked
11. exactly
12. Wales
13. was
14. in the 1850s
15. it
16. A.
17. Western Australia is the largest of Australia's states.
18. Queen Victoria ruled England for many years.

Unit 12A page 34

1. D. See lines 4–5.
2. B. See lines 8–9.
3. C. See lines 12–13.
4. A. You can work out only males were allowed to compete in the ancient festivals whereas all athletes compete in the current Olympics.
5. C. You can work out that Cathy Freeman delivered a torch in the marathon for Australia so the Olympic flame must have been inside it.

6. Answers will vary. You can judge, for example, that they carry on a long tradition, allow athletes to compete with the best in the world and bring nations together in a peaceful way.

Unit 12B page 35

1. Olympic
2. people
3. males
4. gold
5. for example, date, hate, mate, plate, state
6. C.
7. A.
8. Aboriginal
9. international
10. new
11. keep
12. Sydney
13. was
14. at present
15. you
16. B.
17. Female athletes couldn't compete in the past.
18. 'Have you ever been to the Olympics, Mary?' I asked.

Unit 13A page 36

1. C. See line 4.
2. D. See line 14.
3. B. See line 3.
4. B. You can work out Lily has only used one French expression and the rest of her email is in English. Peter is teasing her about this. The smiley face is also a way of showing he isn't serious.
5. A. You can work out it was believed rulers were not treating people fairly because they were thrown into prison just for complaining.
6. C. You can judge that Peter is friendly towards Lily as he writes in a warm-hearted way and helps her out with her question.

Unit 13B page 37

1. celebrated
2. queen
3. banquets
4. fought
5. for example, bought, fought, nought, sought
6. B.
7. D.
8. celebrated
9. improving
10. penniless
11. calm
12. Peter
13. complained
14. on 14 July
15. they
16. C.
17. 'How do they celebrate Bastille Day in France?'
18. The celebrations were held in Paris.

Unit 14A page 38

1. C. See line 4.
2. D. See lines 10–11.
3. C. See line 8.
4. B. You can work out the dog in the water was never really there at all. It was a reflection of the greedy dog.
5. A. You can work out the dog opened his jaws when he jumped into the water. This caused the bone he had stolen to fall out of his mouth.
6. B. You can judge that the story of the greedy dog shows you should be grateful for what you have and not go looking for more.

Unit 14B page 39

1. waste
2. hoped
3. water
4. too
5. for example, bone, cone, done, gone, stone
6. C.
7. A.
8. ashamed
9. nothing
10. appear
11. stare
12. Pridedale
13. glanced
14. immediately
15. we
16. A.
17. Nothing would ever stop him!
18. Warm, cosy, dry and happy, he snuggled in front of the fire.

Unit 15A page 40

1. B. See lines 4–5.
2. C. See line 7.
3. A. See lines 10–12.
4. B. You can work out Akito's family are aware plastic bags can cause the death of sea creatures so they use fewer by switching to canvas bags.
5. C. You can work out that if one car is used to do the work of, say, three cars, then there will be less pollution.
6. D. You can judge that Ms Knight is thoughtful because she listens to her students and then makes a helpful new suggestion to them.

Unit 15B page 41

1. recycling
2. died
3. wrap

4. shopping
5. for example, bull, dull, full, gull, pull
6. B.
7. D.
8. creatures
9. organises
10. hear
11. empty
12. Friskos
13. were
14. each week
15. you
16. A.
17. That's a wonderful idea!
18. You're helping to make a difference.

Revision 2 pages 42–43

1. Rusty, George
2. Antarctica
3. Wales, Abel Tasman, Australia
4. gumboots, puddles, collect, eggs
5. Aboriginal, victory, gold
6. celebration, Bastille Day
7. story, grateful
8. tightly
9. lose
10. males
11. wait
12. queen
13. fought
14. near
15. died
16. wrap
17. never
18. Australia
19. asked
20. in the morning/every morning/at 8 am
21. I
22. you
23. 'What things do you dislike doing?' I asked.
24. She wasn't tall enough to reach the table.
25. I dislike long journeys, new shoes and plastic bags.

NAPLAN-style Reading Test 2 page 44

1. C. See lines 14–15.
2. D. See lines 17–19.
3. D. See lines 7–9.
4. A. You can work out that it is impossible to tell—Sam is a boy's and a girl's name, both girls and boys like high jumping and both boys and girls can be scared of animals.
5. C. You can work out that since getting to Antarctica will involve air and sea travel, Su Lin's dislike of being sick may prevent her from going.
6. A. You can judge Damien swims in a river that dries up in summer. This is likely to be in a country area. No-one else's comments provide any clues as to where they live.

NAPLAN-style Conventions of Language Test 2 page 45

1. high
2. Olympics
3. dries
4. aren't
5. B.
6. C.
7. B.
8. A.
9. B.
10. last year
11. A.
12. D.

Unit 16A page 46

1. B. See line 2.
2. B. See line 8.
3. A. See line 14.
4. B. You can work out that Arachne won the contest because Athena admitted Arachne's tapestry was better than hers.
5. C. You can work out Arachne turned into a spider because she became small with eight legs and was able to spin a web.
6. Answers will vary. It seems unlikely because her father would have been proud of his daughter's talents. He'd not want to hurt her by having her work carelessly destroyed.

Unit 16B page 47

1. crowd
2. boastful
3. better
4. disappeared
5. for example, bell, cell, fell, sell, shell
6. C.
7. A.
8. better
9. contest
10. asked
11. destroyed
12. beautiful
13. past tense
14. slowly
15. because
16. B.
17. She saw her hands had disappeared!
18. 'Do you think her punishment was too harsh?' I asked.

Unit 17A page 48

1. B. See lines 4–5.
2. C. See line 13.
3. A. See line 17.
4. B. You can work out that as the children doing the survey are in Year Three they are likely to be seven, eight or nine years old.

5. D. You can work out the difference is that Liam knows Poppy and Bo well so he refers to them with the names he usually calls them. He uses full names for the other class members he doesn't know as well.
6. C. You can judge Liam found the survey results interesting because he paid a lot of attention to them and wrote about them in detail.

Unit 17B page 49

1. surveys
2. born
3. travelling
4. years
5. for example, flap, gap, lap, map, slap
6. C.
7. A.
8. visited
9. travelling
10. foe
11. dreary
12. good
13. future tense
14. by plane
15. but
16. B.
17. He has been to Adelaide, Darwin and Melbourne.
18. I asked which places she had visited.

Unit 18A page 50

1. C. See line 8.
2. C. See lines 10–13.
3. A. See line 15.
4. C. You can work out she is talking about a seahorse because she is riding a seahorse in the picture and seahorses live in the sea.
5. D. You can work out the narrator is annoyed about having feet because you need a tail to be a mermaid.
6. B. You can judge the narrator is having fun imagining a different life but she is not at all serious about becoming a mermaid as she knows it is impossible.

Unit 18B page 51

1. tail
2. bored
3. horse
4. nuisance
5. for example, fail, hail, mail, nail, rail
6. A.
7. B.
8. surrounded
9. nuisance
10. demand
11. found
12. blue
13. past tense
14. together
15. and
16. C.
17. 'I wouldn't do that if I were you.'
18. 'Don't ever say that!'

Unit 19A page 52

1. B. See lines 2–4.
2. A. See the chart.
3. D. See line 14.
4. B. You can work out Jason knows farms and dams attract insects. He mentions this to further explain why he was able to find so many insects.
5. D. You can work out he stopped counting because there were so many ants that he felt he'd never be able to count them all.
6. A. You can judge Jason is very interested because he took a lot of trouble searching and recording his findings about insects and he knows about their habits.

Unit 19B page 53

1. Congratulations
2. weekend
3. pairs
4. biting
5. for example, bee, flee, free, tree, agree
6. A.
7. D.
8. wonder
9. remember
10. good
11. hold
12. jointed
13. past tense
14. patiently
15. because
16. B.
17. Nan's house is quite close to ours.
18. Dad said, 'Did you know ladybirds have wings?'

Unit 20A page 54

1. C. See line 7.
2. C. See lines 4–5.
3. D. See line 8.
4. B. You can work out the emu's wings are very small and they are very large birds. It seems likely that their wings can't lift their weight.
5. B. You can work out that emus have some predators who chase them so they need to be able to run quickly in order to escape them.

Answers

6. D. You can judge the text is an information report as it presents factual information about a class of birds.

Unit 20B page 55

1. height
2. beaks
3. feathers
4. predator
5. for example, hide, ride, side, tide
6. D.
7. A.
8. direction
9. assets
10. shaggy
11. several
12. three
13. present tense
14. speedily/quickly
15. because
16. B.
17. Emus' feathers are brownish in colour.
18. An emu's wings are smaller than a crow's.

Unit 21A page 56

1. C. See lines 4–5.
2. D. See line 13.
3. C. See line 14.
4. A. You can work out Hook thinks the crocodile got a taste for him when it ate his arm.
5. B. You can work out Hook wants to get his revenge on Peter Pan who he thinks caused the crocodile to get a taste of him.
6. C. You can judge that Hook is full of anger when he 'barks' at Smee and tells him he wants to catch Peter. His voice quivers with nervousness when he thinks of the danger he is in.

Unit 21B page 57

1. crocodile
2. following
3. licked
4. lucky
5. for example, kick, pick, sick, tick, stick
6. A.
7. C.
8. lucky
9. corrected
10. whispered
11. stayed
12. large
13. future tense
14. huskily
15. because
16. B.
17. 'One day,' said Peter, 'Hook will make a mistake.'
18. 'Do you have a dread of crocodiles?'

Unit 22A page 58

1. B. See lines 3–4.
2. C. See line 12.
3. D. See lines 13–15.
4. C. You can work out they are more than ten because they have been guarding penguins for ten years and would have to have trained as young dogs for some time before that.
5. B. You can work out the idea of using Maremmas to guard penguins had never been thought of or tried anywhere else in the world.
6. Answers will vary. You can judge that a world-first Australian idea being successful is newsworthy. Similarly, a story about animals protecting animals that can't protect themselves would have appeal for news readers.

Unit 22B page 59

1. guarded
2. penguin
3. farmer
4. council
5. for example, bark, dark, lark, mark, shark
6. D.
7. C.
8. attack
9. idea
10. concluded
11. remembered
12. free-range
13. present tense
14. successfully
15. or
16. A.
17. Maremmas are native to Italy.
18. 'I'd love to see a baby Maremma.'

Revision 3 pages 60-61

1. eight, hairy
2. baby, blue
3. old, white, pretty
4. destroy, finished
5. wish, swallow
6. found, cook, surprise
7. remember, got
8. years
9. bored
10. tales
11. nuisance
12. weekend
13. advertisement
14. guarded
15. council
16. wait
17. definitely
18. glared
19. harmless
20. were
21. quickly
22. because
23. 'She'd love to visit Japan.'

24. 'Do they make good guard dogs?' asked the farmer.
25. 'Don't swim there because there are crocodiles in the water!'

NAPLAN-style Reading Test 3 page 62

1. D. See line 2.
2. A. See lines 6–7.
3. B. See line 8.
4. C. You can work out his mother thought Jack was silly because he'd wasted this chance of selling the cow to get money to buy them food.
5. D. You can work out the words the giant bellows about eating children are to threaten Jack and make him afraid he'll be eaten by the giant.
6. C. You can judge that without the golden egg Jack's family would not have had money for food.

NAPLAN-style Conventions of Language Test 3 page 63

1. money
2. offered
3. beanstalks
4. immediately
5. C.
6. A.
7. C.
8. A.
9. immediately
10. swiftly
11. D.
12. B.

Unit 23A page 64

1. A. See lines 2–3.
2. B. See line 14.
3. B. See lines 7–8.
4. A. You can work out the five pairs of false legs might trick you into thinking a caterpillar couldn't be an insect.
5. D. You can work out a butterfly's egg must turn into a caterpillar so the cycle can begin again.
6. C. You can judge it is unusual for any living thing to change into something that looks and behaves quite differently from what it once was.

Unit 23B page 65

1. caterpillar
2. muscles
3. weight
4. cocoon
5. for example, dumps, lumps, humps, pumps, stumps
6. C.
7. A.
8. weight
9. surfaces
10. real
11. whole
12. a long, soft body
13. see
14. hungrily
15. but
16. B.
17. She saw a cocoon hanging from a branch.
18. 'Do you remember that book with holes in the pages?'

Unit 24A page 66

1. A. See line 4.
2. C. See line 11.
3. D. See line 7.
4. B. You can work out the stuffing is needed to fill out the shirt so it looks as if the scarecrow is a person with a body.
5. D. You can work out that the bird sitting on the scarecrow's arm proves it has failed to do its job successfully.
6. Answers will vary. You are likely to judge it to be easy if you understand all the instructions and have done that kind of thing before. If not, you could disagree by pointing out it has too many steps, is too difficult and is very complicated.

Unit 24B page 67

1. scare
2. length
3. hole
4. screw
5. for example, bead, dead, lead, read, bread
6. B.
7. C.
8. away
9. through
10. frighten
11. separate
12. the wooden structure
13. pin
14. easily
15. and
16. A.
17. 'Why don't you use buttons for the eyes?'
18. That scarecrow couldn't scare anything!

Answers

Unit 25A page 68

1. B. See line 2.
2. C. See line 11.
3. A. See line 9.
4. B. You can work out that Harry thinks computers make things such as getting information and keeping in touch with friends easier to do.
5. D. You can work out that Jasmine only has negative things to say about computers so she would argue computers don't improve her life.
6. B. You can judge Jasmine's first comment makes a good point but her second is more of a personal preference. This makes her comments only somewhat convincing.

Unit 25B page 69

1. everything
2. information
3. pieces
4. research
5. for example, bind, kind, mind, rind, wind
6. C.
7. A.
8. computer
9. research
10. uncertain
11. fact
12. a best friend
13. talk
14. on the computer
15. or
16. A.
17. 'Do you agree with what I said?'
18. Stella answered, 'Yes, I do.'

Unit 26A page 70

1. C. See line 2.
2. B. See line 7.
3. C. See line 14.
4. A. You can work out that Alice has grown so large she can't fit into the spaces she wants to be in. It means her tears are also enormous and almost cause a flood.
5. D. You can work out she hopes to shame herself into not crying any more by speaking very crossly to herself.
6. B. You can judge the author feels sorry for Alice. He says 'Poor Alice!' and he describes what happens to her in a very understanding way.

Unit 26B page 71

1. feet
2. hopeless
3. ought
4. gallons
5. for example, bears, fears, gears, hears, spears
6. B.
7. C.
8. fact
9. hopeless
10. continue
11. less
12. the little golden key
13. look
14. at once
15. and
16. C.
17. The tears shed by Alice soon made a deep pool.
18. 'Stop that crying at once!'

Unit 27A page 72

1. C. See lines 11–12.
2. D. See lines 12–13.
3. B. See line 17.
4. D. You can work out clans cared for their land and knew to move to another area when they had used its resources so it could recover and be used again by others.
5. B. You can work out that the strong connection between Aboriginal people and the land is a spiritual one. They believe themselves to be part of it and it part of them.
6. C. You can judge that the sculpture of Bunjil represents the totem Bunjil. It is a way for the people of Melbourne to show they recognise that area once belonged to the Wurundjeri.

Unit 27B page 73

1. language
2. animals
3. city
4. eagle
5. for example, band, hand, sand, wand
6. A.
7. A.
8. tribes
9. customs
10. individuals
11. doubts
12. The Wurundjeri
13. is
14. silently
15. and
16. B.
17. 'Have you seen Bunjil the eagle in Melbourne?'
18. Aboriginal people share many beliefs.

Answers

Unit 28A page 74

1. C. See line 8.
2. D. See line 11.
3. A. See line 9.
4. B. You can work out the figures in skirts represent females and the figures without skirts represent males.
5. B. You can work out these two censuses were taken 100 years apart. Almost everything has changed over that time.
6. Answers may vary. You can judge that it would be easier to add answers together if they are already on a computer. It would save the government time and money.

Unit 28B page 75

1. census
2. people
3. questions
4. compulsory
5. for example, bill, hill, pill, will, spill
6. A.
7. C.
8. national
9. statistics
10. separate
11. double
12. paper censuses
13. are
14. on 2 April 1911
15. or
16. C.
17. People fill in the census with paper and pen.
18. Until 2016, the census was not filled in online.

Unit 29A page 76

1. C. See lines 7–8.
2. A. See line 5.
3. C. See line 6.
4. C. You can work out the word 'here' in line 4 refers to China. Auntie Changchang lives there and knows about the customs and traditions of Chinese New Year celebrations.
5. A. You can work out Amy is doing a project about Chinese New Year because Auntie Changchang wishes her good luck with it after giving her lots of detailed information on the subject.
6. D. You can judge the information given is first-hand as Auntie Changchang lives where the celebrations take place. She sounds knowledgeable, observant and trustworthy.

Unit 29B page 77

1. paper
2. celebrations
3. population
4. Dragon
5. for example, fight, might, night, right, sight
6. B.
7. A.
8. decorate
9. population
10. disagreeable
11. friends
12. pretty, red paper-cutouts
13. celebrate
14. from top to bottom
15. so
16. B.
17. Auntie Changchang sent me a postcard.
18. I hope I did well in my project.

Unit 30A page 78

1. D. See lines 6–7.
2. B. See line 8.
3. C. See lines 10–11.
4. D. You can work out Dot's father didn't know Dot was in the Kangaroo's pouch. He had been watching for the Kangaroo, with his gun in hand, waiting to shoot it.
5. C. You can work out Dot's father is delighted to see her safe and alive after he had nearly shot her by mistake.
6. A. You can judge the author disapproves because she describes Dot's father's gun as 'cruel' and shows what fatal damage could be done with it by mistake.

Unit 30B page 79

1. bounded
2. noise
3. pouch
4. fear
5. for example, been, green, queen, teen, between
6. D.
7. C.
8. lightning
9. fatal
10. brave
11. silence
12. The kangaroo
13. cried
14. blindly
15. but
16. C.
17. The Kangaroo watched Dot run to her father.
18. 'Help!' shouted Jack.

Answers

Revision 4 pages 80-81

1. a census
2. a hairy, green caterpillar
3. the pretty decorations
4. used, crops
5. cocoon, butterfly
6. ashamed, moment
7. comfortably, home
8. emails
9. animals
10. hole
11. cruel
12. paper
13. hopeless
14. celebration
15. population
16. knew
17. fact
18. The body
19. is/was
20. in the refrigerator/in the icebox/in the freezer
21. because
22. or
23. Scarecrows are fun to make.
24. 'Why don't you disappear?' asked Alice.
25. 'Look out!' Jack yelled.

NAPLAN-style Reading Test 4 page 82

1. C. See line 12.
2. C. See lines 5–6.
3. A. See lines 13–14.
4. D. You can work out Chilli's family does tourist activities such as go to exhibitions and travel on a tourist tram. This suggests they are having a holiday. The title of the text also says they are on holiday.
5. A. You can work out the smiley face is a way of showing she is making a joke about the Yarra as many people do. It may look brown and muddy but it is still a famous landmark people like to visit.
6. B. You can judge that Chilli's relationship with her gran is loving from the way she shares things with her and the warm, affectionate way she writes to her.

NAPLAN-style Conventions of Language Test 4 page 83

1. guess
2. eagle
3. advertisement
4. enormous
5. C.
6. C.
7. D.
8. family
9. C.
10. B.
11. C.
12. A.

Vocabulary

16 Circle the correct word in the brackets.
Please use bubble (rap / wrap) around that glass.

17 Circle the word that does **not** belong.
usually mostly never normally

Grammar

18 Add a proper noun to the sentence.
Canberra is the capital of ______________________.

19 Add a saying verb to the sentence.
I ______________________ a question about the date of Bastille Day.

20 Add a prepositional phrase to tell **when**.
I eat my breakfast ______________________.

21 Add a pronoun to the sentence.
Mum told me to use a booster seat but ______________________ didn't want to use one.

22 Add a pronoun to the sentence.
If I give you my gumboots will ______________________ look after them, please?

Punctuation

Rewrite each sentence correctly.

23 What things do you dislike doing? I asked.

____

____

24 she wasnt tall enough to reach the table

____

____

25 I dislike long journeys new shoes and plastic bags.

____

____

Reading

Likes and dislikes

Damien

I like:
anything that is green, especially trees, grass, broccoli and spinach.

I dislike:
the heat in summer because it dries up the river where we swim.

Sally

I like:
to read books—sad or funny, with pictures or without—of any kind really.

I dislike:
scary movies. I shut my eyes in the scary parts but I can still hear the music playing loudly.

Sam

I like:
competing in the high jump at school. I saw the event at the Olympic Games last year.

I dislike:
our neighbour's cat. It hisses at me when I try to pat it.

Su Lin

I like:
learning about Antarctica. I want to visit there when I grow up.

I dislike:
flying in aeroplanes because I get airsick. I also get seasick.

1 Who has been to the Olympics?
- A Damien
- B Sally
- C Sam
- D Su Lin

2 Why does Su Lin dislike flying?
- A She gets scared.
- B She gets hot.
- C She gets tired.
- D She gets airsick.

3 What kind of books does Sally like?
- A scary
- B picture
- C sad
- D any

4 Is Sam a girl or a boy?
- A There is no evidence to tell whether Sam is a girl or a boy.
- B You can tell she's a girl because she's scared of cats.
- C You can tell from his name he's a boy.
- D You can tell he's a boy because he likes high jumping.

5 What might stop Su Lin going to Antarctica when she grows up?
- A It may be too expensive.
- B She'd rather go to the Olympics.
- C fear of getting airsick and seasick
- D She might be too busy.

6 Which person is the most likely to be living in the country?
- A Damien
- B Sally
- C Sam
- D Su Lin

NAPLAN-STYLE

2

CONVENTIONS OF LANGUAGE TEST

Spelling

The spelling mistakes in these sentences have been underlined.
Write the correct spelling on the lines.

1. I was in the long jump and the hygh jump at the sports carnival. ______________________

2. I wish I could go to the Olimpics. ______________________

3. Our creek drys up in summer too. ______________________

4. You ar'ent the only one who likes books. ______________________

Vocabulary

5. Which word means **especially**?
   A oddly **B** particularly **C** mostly **D** even

6. Which word does **not** belong?
   A scary **B** frightening **C** soothing **D** spooky

7. Which word does **not** belong?
   A learn **B** teach **C** study **D** research

Grammar

8. Which is the proper noun in this sentence?
   Sam collected stamps, maps and football jumpers.
   A Sam **B** stamps **C** maps **D** football

9. Which is the verb in this sentence?
   Sally and Su Lin read plenty of books.
   A Sally **B** read **C** plenty **D** books

10. Which words tell **when**?
    Sam saw the Olympic Games last year. ______________________

Punctuation

11. Which sentence is punctuated correctly?
    A Sam said, 'I don't like scary movies either.'
    B Sam said 'I don't like scary movies either.'
    C Sam said 'I dont like scary movies either.'
    D sam said, 'I don't like scary movies either.'

12. Which sentence is punctuated correctly?
    A These are a few of my favourite things!
    B These are a few of my favourite things?
    C these are a few of my favourite things!
    D These are a few of my favourite things.

Reading and Comprehension

The spider woman

Arachne wove the most beautiful tapestries. They were admired by everyone.

'My tapestries are the best in the world. I need no help from the Goddess Athena,' she boasted.

'Do you think you are better than Athena?' asked an old woman in rags who was among the crowd.

'Certainly,' replied Arachne.

'Then let us have a contest,' said the old woman. Her rags fell away and Athena was revealed.

'I told you I was better,' Arachne said proudly as their tapestries were compared.

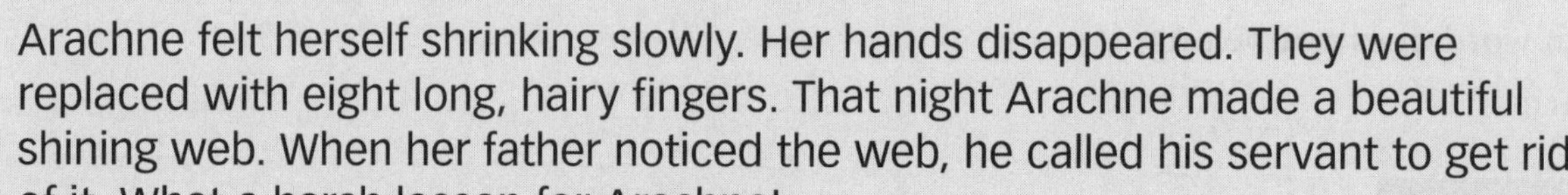

'You may be better but you are without respect. You need to be taught a lesson,' the Goddess replied.

Arachne felt herself shrinking slowly. Her hands disappeared. They were replaced with eight long, hairy fingers. That night Arachne made a beautiful shining web. When her father noticed the web, he called his servant to get rid of it. What a harsh lesson for Arachne!

Adapted from a Greek myth

1. The tapestries Arachne wove were
   - **A** large.
   - **B** beautiful.
   - **C** shining.
   - **D** brightly coloured.
2. Who said they should have a contest?
   - **A** Arachne's father
   - **B** the old woman
   - **C** Arachne
   - **D** the spider
3. What happened to Arachne after the contest?
   - **A** She shrank.
   - **B** She made a new tapestry.
   - **C** She talked to her father.
   - **D** She said she was sorry.
4. Who won the weaving contest?
   - **A** the old woman
   - **B** Arachne
   - **C** Athena
   - **D** Arachne's father
5. What did Arachne turn into?
   - **A** a tapestry
   - **B** a spider's web
   - **C** a spider
   - **D** a servant
6. Do you think Arachne's father knew she made the web?

Spelling

Rewrite the misspelt words.

1 The croud was getting restless.

2 Arachne was very boastfull.

3 I think your tapestry is beter than mine.

4 She dissapeared before my eyes!

5 Change the first letter of **tell** to make three new words.

Vocabulary

Circle the word that has the nearest meaning to the underlined word.

6 Arachne boasted about her talents.

- **A** strutted
- **B** exaggerated
- **C** bragged
- **D** smiled

7 You have to admire her talent.

- **A** praise
- **B** understand
- **C** see
- **D** blame

8 Add a word from the text to the sentence.

I am much ______ than you are at this game.

9 Write a word from the text to match the meaning.

event in which people compete

Circle the word on each line that does **not** belong.

10 replied remarked asked answered

11 made destroyed created shaped

Grammar

12 Complete the sentence with an adjective from the text.

'I make the most ______ tapestries,' said Arachne.

13 Which tense is the underlined verb in this sentence?

I told you I was the better weaver.

14 Write an adverb from the text to tell **how**.

She found she was turning ______ into a spider.

15 Choose a conjunction from the box to complete the sentence correctly.

and	so	but	because	or

Arachne was punished ______ she was without respect.

Punctuation

16 Circle the sentence that is punctuated correctly.

- **A** 'My tapestries are the best there are' said Athena.
- **B** 'My tapestries are the best there are,' said Athena.
- **C** 'My tapestries are the best there are', said Athena.

Rewrite each sentence correctly.

17 She saw her hands had disappeared

18 'Do you think her punishment was too harsh,' I asked.

Where have you been?

We did a survey in our class about which places we had lived in or visited. James Cook said he had been to Texas, Singapore and Melbourne. He showed us those places on a world map. Emily Sharp had visited four Australian states and the Northern Territory. She said she loves travelling by plane. No-one in our Year Three class had been to as many places in Australia as she had.

My good friend Poppy lived in Port Moresby, New Guinea, for two years and then in the mountains at Mount Hagen for another two years. Another friend, Bo, was born in Beijing. His family moved here from China when he was one.

We have to give a talk about where we would like to visit and why. I want to snorkel at the Great Barrier Reef in Queensland one day because I think the coral would be spectacular.

By Liam

1. Who had been to Singapore?
   - **A** Emily
   - **B** James
   - **C** Poppy
   - **D** Bo

2. Who lived in New Guinea?
   - **A** Emily
   - **B** James
   - **C** Poppy
   - **D** Bo

3. In which state is the Great Barrier Reef?
   - **A** Queensland
   - **B** Western Australia
   - **C** Tasmania
   - **D** New South Wales

4. About how old are the children who did the survey?
   - **A** two to five
   - **B** seven to nine
   - **C** twelve to fifteen
   - **D** adult

5. Liam doesn't give Poppy and Bo's surnames because
   - **A** he has never heard them.
   - **B** he forgot to add them.
   - **C** he can't spell them.
   - **D** they are his friends.

6. Liam found the results of the survey
   - **A** boring.
   - **B** inaccurate.
   - **C** interesting.
   - **D** confusing.

Spelling

Rewrite the misspelt words.

1 You find out interesting things from sirveys.

2 I was borne in Sydney, New South Wales.

3 She doesn't like traveling by car.

4 Did you live there for two yeers?

5 Change the first letter of **cap** to make three new words.

Vocabulary

Circle the word that has the nearest meaning to the underlined word.

6 James has been to many different places.

A countless B few

C numerous D some

7 We marked the places on a world map.

A global B large

C country D real

8 Add a word from the text to the sentence.

Have you ever ______ Uluru in the Northern Territory?

9 Write a word from the text to match the meaning.

going from one place to another

Circle the word on each line that does **not** belong.

10 playmate foe friend companion

11 spectacular amazing dreary magnificent

Grammar

12 Complete the sentence with an adjective from the text.

I have two ______ friends in my class at school.

13 Which tense is the underlined verb in this sentence?

It will be fun to snorkel next week.

14 Write a prepositional phrase from the text to tell **how**.

I have never travelled

______.

15 Choose a conjunction from the box to complete the sentence correctly.

and	so	but	because	or

Poppy lives here now ______ she used to live in New Guinea.

Punctuation

16 Circle the sentence that is punctuated correctly.

A She was born in Beijing China.

B She was born in Beijing, China.

C She was born in Beijing, China!

Rewrite each sentence correctly.

17 He has been to Adelaide, Darwin, and Melbourne!

18 I asked which places she had visited?

Reading and Comprehension

I wish I were a mermaid

I wish I were a mermaid
living in the deep.
I'd dive and swim and swish my tail.
I'd never need to sleep.

I wouldn't need a home,
a place of bricks and mortar.
Instead I'd dwell in a beautiful shell—
surrounded by blue water.

If I grew bored and lonely
which I wouldn't do, of course,
I'd look around until I found
a playful, prancing 'horse.

We'd ride the waves together,
find tasty fish to eat.
Oh yes! I know I'd love it—such a
nuisance having feet!

1. What would the mermaid's dwelling be made from?
   - **A** the waves
   - **B** a seahorse
   - **C** a shell
   - **D** the deep

2. The mermaid would look for a 'horse when she was
   - **A** tired.
   - **B** hungry.
   - **C** lonely.
   - **D** sleepy.

3. What would the mermaid eat?
   - **A** fish
   - **B** 'horses
   - **C** shells
   - **D** waves

4. What kind of 'horse does the mermaid mean?
   - **A** a pony
   - **B** a racehorse
   - **C** a seahorse
   - **D** a draught horse

5. The narrator complains about her feet because
   - **A** they get in her way.
   - **B** they get in her 'horse's way.
   - **C** they hurt.
   - **D** they stop her being a mermaid.

6. The poem is mainly
   - **A** serious and grim.
   - **B** lighthearted and fun.
   - **C** scary and worrying.
   - **D** sad and upsetting.

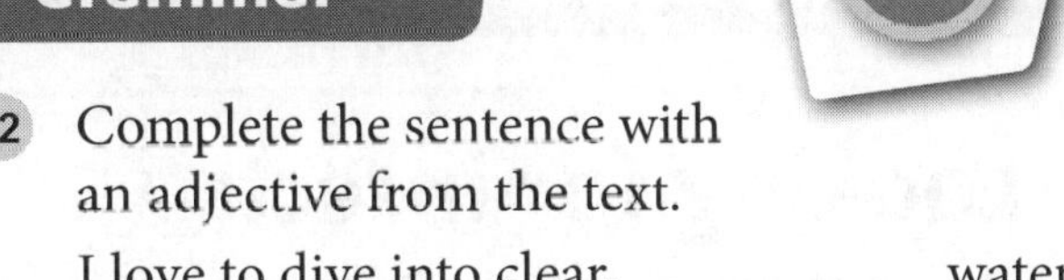

Spelling

Rewrite the misspelt words.

1 The mermaid sat on a rock and spread out her tale.

2 I get board easily.

3 Have you ever ridden a hoarse?

4 Ms Brown said I was being a newsance.

5 Change the first letter of **tail** to make three new words.

Vocabulary

Circle the word that has the nearest meaning to the underlined word.

6 Mermaids are good at flouncing their tails.
A swishing **B** wagging
C displaying **D** flinging

7 When my friends go away I feel lonely.
A thirsty **B** friendless
C gloomy **D** dismal

8 Add a word from the text to the sentence.
When I swim I am ______ by the ocean.

9 Write a word from the text to match the meaning.
someone or something that makes you feel annoyed ______

Circle the word on each line that does **not** belong.

10 hope want wish demand

11 searched found hunted explored

Grammar

12 Complete the sentence with an adjective from the text.
I love to dive into clear, ______ water.

13 Which tense is the underlined verb in this sentence?
If I were a mermaid, I would never sleep.

14 Write an adverb from the text to tell **how**.
We could ride ______ on the waves.

15 Choose a conjunction from the box to complete the sentence correctly.

and	so	but	because	or

Our house is made of bricks ______ mortar.

Punctuation

16 Circle the sentence that is punctuated correctly.
A They love to dive and swim, in the ocean.
B They love to dive, and swim, in the ocean.
C They love to dive and swim in the ocean.

Rewrite each sentence correctly.

17 'I wouldnt do that if I were you.'

18 'Don't ever say that.'

UNIT 19A

Reading and Comprehension

Looking for insects

'Congratulations, Year Three. Your homework about the insects you observed over the weekend was well done.

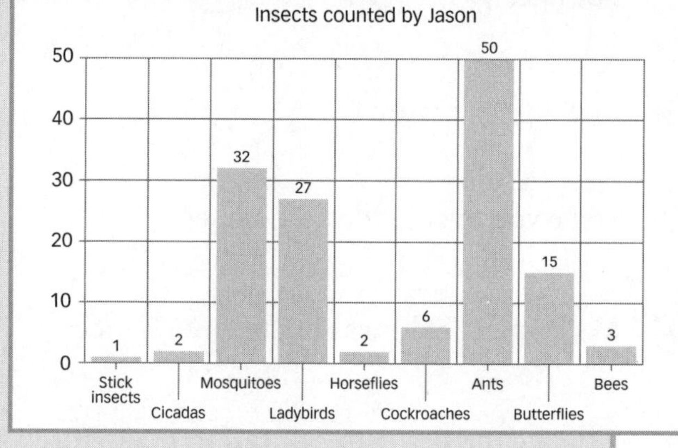

Jason saw the most insects: 138. I wonder why? And he didn't include spiders! Remember insects have a three-part body, three pairs of jointed legs, compound eyes and one pair of antennae.

Would you tell us about your observations please, Jason?'

'I made a chart to record my observations. I spent ages patiently looking for insects so that might be why I saw so many. Also we live on a farm near a dam. I found a stick insect hanging on a wall behind our shed. The horseflies (they breed in cattle manure) flew through the window of our car when we were driving to my nan's. They kept trying to bite my legs. And I gave up when I got to fifty ants!'

1. Year Three's homework was about
   - **A** the weekend.
   - **B** the number of insects they saw.
   - **C** where they live.
   - **D** making a chart.

2. How many stick insects did Jason see?
   - **A** one
   - **B** fifty
   - **C** 138
   - **D** none

3. Where did Jason record his observations?
   - **A** on the whiteboard
   - **B** on his phone
   - **C** in his head
   - **D** on a chart

4. Jason says, 'Also we live on a farm near a dam' to explain
   - **A** how proud he is of his home.
   - **B** why he saw so many insects.
   - **C** that there are animals on farms.
   - **D** that there is manure where he lives.

5. Why did Jason give up when he got to fifty ants?
   - **A** It was bedtime.
   - **B** He had to go to his nan's.
   - **C** He was tired.
   - **D** They seemed countless.

6. How interested is Jason in insects?
   - **A** very
   - **B** not very
   - **C** quite
   - **D** not at all

Spelling

Rewrite the misspelt words.

1 Congratulatens on your very good work, Millie.

2 We had some homework to do last weakend.

3 Insects have three pears of jointed legs.

4 The flies kept bighting my legs.

5 Change the first letter of **see** to make three new words.

Vocabulary

Circle the word that has the nearest meaning to the underlined word.

6 Did you see any spiders in the garden?
A notice B watch
C study D miss

7 I recorded the information on this chart.
A gave B scribbled
C read D reported

8 Add a word from the text to the sentence.
Do you ever ______ if insects dream?

9 Write a word from the text to match the meaning.
bring something back to your mind

Circle the word on each line that does **not** belong.

10 bad weak good poor

11 bite hold nip sting

Grammar

12 Complete the sentence with an adjective from the text.
Insects have three pairs of ______ legs.

13 Which tense is the underlined verb in this sentence?
Jason saw the most insects.

14 Write an adverb from the text to tell **how**.
Jason spent a long time ______ looking for insects.

15 Choose a conjunction from the box to complete the sentence correctly.

and	so	but	because	or

That looks like an insect ______ it has six legs and three body parts.

Punctuation

16 Circle the sentence that is punctuated correctly.
A Horseflies hurt when they bite
B Horseflies hurt when they bite.
C horseflies hurt when they bite

Rewrite each sentence correctly.

17 Nans house is quite close to ours.

18 Dad said, 'Did you know ladybirds have wings.

Reading and Comprehension

Emus

Emus are Australia's largest native bird. They are only found in Australia. They are tall birds and can reach two metres in height. The emu and the kangaroo are on Australia's coat of arms.

Emus' feathers are shaggy and brownish. Their necks and heads are almost bald. They use their wide beaks for eating seeds and grasses. An emu does have wings but they are smaller than a crow's!

Their three toes have flattened pads underneath. This helps them to run fast over rough ground. They are the only birds with calf muscles in their legs. These assets allow them to reach speeds of around 50 km/h.

Their main predators are wild cats, wedge-tailed eagles, dingoes and humans. Cats can outrun emus but emus have a clever trick up their sleeves. They raise one wing and lower the other, speedily swivel 180 degrees and then change direction. The cats can't turn as quickly as this so the emus gain a chance to escape.

1 What colour are an emu's feathers?
- **A** bluish
- **B** whitish
- **C** brownish
- **D** greyish

2 What height can emus reach?
- **A** one metre
- **B** one and a half metres
- **C** two metres
- **D** two and a half metres

3 Which parts of an emu are almost bald?
- **A** necks
- **B** heads
- **C** calf muscles
- **D** necks and heads

4 What is a reason emus can't fly?
- **A** They can run very fast.
- **B** Their wings are too small to carry their weight.
- **C** They have lots of feathers.
- **D** They have never wanted to fly.

5 Why do emus need to run quickly?
- **A** to hunt for food
- **B** to escape from predators
- **C** to display their wings
- **D** to use their toes

6 What kind of text is 'Emus'?
- **A** a media release
- **B** a prescription
- **C** a narrative
- **D** an information report

Spelling

Rewrite the misspelt words.

1 What hight do they reach?

2 Emus have beeks that are rather wide.

3 Their fethers are shaggy.

4 An eagle would be a frightening preddater.

5 Change the first letter of **wide** to make three new words.

Vocabulary

Circle the word that has the nearest meaning to the underlined word.

6 Emus are able to run over rough ground.
A uncomfortable B wild
C violent D uneven

7 Wild cats can outrun emus.
A overtake B follow
C outplay D conquer

8 Add a word from the text to the sentence.
Emus are able to change ______ quickly when being chased.

9 Write a word from the text to match the meaning.
useful qualities ______

Circle the word on each line that does **not** belong.

10 smooth, velvety, shaggy, shaven

11 several, only, particular, lone

Grammar

12 Complete the sentence with an adjective from the text.
Emus have ______ toes.

13 Which tense is the underlined verb in this sentence?
The emu and kangaroo are on our coat of arms.

14 Write an adverb from the text to tell **how**.
Emus swivel their bodies ______ to escape from wild cats.

15 Choose a conjunction from the box to complete the sentence correctly.

and	so	but	because	or

Emus can't fly partly ______ their wings are too small.

Punctuation

16 Circle the sentence that is punctuated correctly.
A Theres an emu on the Australian coat of arms.
B There's an emu on the Australian coat of arms.
C There's an emu on the Australian Coat of Arms.

Rewrite each sentence correctly.

17 emus feathers are brownish in colour

18 An emu's wings are smaller than a crows.

Reading and Comprehension

Captain Hook

'I have often,' said Smee, 'noticed your strange dread of crocodiles.'

'Not of crocodiles,' Hook corrected him, 'but of that one crocodile.' He lowered his voice. 'It liked my arm so much, Smee, that it has followed me ever since, from sea to sea and from land to land, licking its lips for the rest of me.'

'In a way,' said Smee, 'it's sort of a compliment.'

'I want no such compliments,' Hook barked petulantly. 'I want Peter Pan, who first gave the brute its taste for me.'

He sat down on a large mushroom, and now there was a quiver in his voice. 'Smee,' he said huskily, 'that crocodile would have had me before this, but by a lucky chance it swallowed a clock which goes tick tick inside it, and so before it can reach me I hear the tick and bolt.' ...

'Some day,' said Smee, 'the clock will run down, and then he'll get you.'

Extract from *Peter Pan* by JM Barrie, 1905

1. What does Captain Hook dread?
   - **A** crocodiles
   - **B** his hook
   - **C** one crocodile
   - **D** ticking clocks

2. What is Peter's surname?
   - **A** Smee
   - **B** Hook
   - **C** Barrie
   - **D** Pan

3. What did Hook sit down on?
   - **A** an arm
   - **B** a crocodile
   - **C** a mushroom
   - **D** a clock

4. Hook thinks the crocodile follows him because
   - **A** it likes the taste of him.
   - **B** it likes frightening him.
   - **C** it is attracted to hooks.
   - **D** it prefers his taste to Peter Pan's.

5. Captain Hook wants Peter Pan so he can
   - **A** reward him.
   - **B** punish him.
   - **C** thank him.
   - **D** introduce him to Smee.

6. Captain Hook is
   - **A** thoughtful and gentle.
   - **B** terrifying and evil.
   - **C** angry and nervous.
   - **D** bold and heroic.

Spelling

Rewrite the misspelt words.

1 Never smile at a crockodile!

2 I'm sure someone was folowing me.

3 The crocodile liked his lips as he dreamt of Captain Hook.

4 I was a luky duck!

5 Change the first letter of **lick** to make three new words.

Vocabulary

Circle the word that has the nearest meaning to the underlined word.

6 His voice quivered nervously when he spoke.

A trembled B twinkled
C pulsed D throbbed

7 'Get away from here right now,' he shouted petulantly.

A kindly B sweetly
C crossly D patiently

8 Add a word from the text to the sentence.
I had a ______
escape from that crocodile.

9 Write a word from the text to match the meaning.
put right ______

Circle the word on each line that does **not** belong.

10 yelled barked shouted whispered

11 ran bolted stayed fled

Grammar

12 Complete the sentence with an adjective from the text.
There was a tiny clock ticking inside a ______ crocodile.

13 Which tense is the underlined verb group in this sentence?
One day that clock will stop!

14 Write an adverb from the text to tell **how**.
He spoke ______
to Smee as he confessed his fears.

15 Choose a conjunction from the box to complete the sentence correctly.

and	so	but	because	or

Hook was afraid ______
he knew the crocodile was after him.

Punctuation

16 Circle the sentence that is punctuated correctly.

A Hook said 'I'll catch him yet!'.
B Hook said, 'I'll catch him yet!'
C Hook said, 'Ill catch him yet!'

Rewrite each sentence correctly.

17 'One day' said Peter 'Hook will make a mistake.

18 'Do you have a dread of crocodiles!'

Reading and Comprehension

Middle Island News

Goodbye Eudy and Tula

For ten years Eudy and Tula, Maremma sheepdogs, have guarded a penguin colony in Victoria's south-west. They have kept the penguins safe from attack by foxes during the breeding season.

The scheme, a world-first to use Maremmas in this way, was hatched in 2006. It was the brainwave of a local chicken farmer, Swampy Marsh. At the time, Swampy was successfully using Maremmas to watch over his free-range chickens. He suggested trying them out as guardians for the penguins. The council and other supporters raised the funds.

Eudy and Tula, Maremma sheepdog sisters, received intensive training for the job. When they began their work there were fewer than ten pairs of breeding penguins left in the colony. Now numbers are nearer the 200 mark. But at last it is time for the two dogs to retire.

The good news is that they are to be replaced by two new penguin protectors.

1. Eudy and Tula are
   - **A** brothers.
   - **B** sisters.
   - **C** cousins.
   - **D** not related.

2. Who is Swampy Marsh?
   - **A** a dog trainer
   - **B** a penguin protector
   - **C** a chicken farmer
   - **D** a newspaper editor

3. Eudy and Tula are being farewelled because
   - **A** they want to work for Swampy Marsh.
   - **B** they are sick and tired of their job.
   - **C** they have saved lots of penguins.
   - **D** it is time for them to retire.

4. How old are Eudy and Tula?
   - **A** not yet ten
   - **B** exactly ten
   - **C** more than ten
   - **D** no-one knows

5. It was a **world-first** idea because sheepdogs
   - **A** had not guarded penguins in Australia before.
   - **B** had never been used to guard penguins.
   - **C** only knew how to guard chickens.
   - **D** already knew how to guard sheep.

6. What makes this story newsworthy?

Spelling

Rewrite the misspelt words.

1 In Italy, Maremma sheepdogs have garded stock for a long time.

....

2 Look at that beautiful baby pengun!

....

3 I want to be a falmer when I grow up.

....

4 The local cowncil was helpful with the project.

....

5 Change the first letter of **park** to make three new words.

....

....

....

Vocabulary

Circle the word that has the nearest meaning to the underlined word.

6 The penguin colony is well guarded by the sheepdogs.

A followed **B** sheltered
C disguised **D** protected

7 Crowdfunding raised much of the money they needed.

A lifted **B** enlarged
C made **D** used

8 Add a word from the text to the sentence.

Penguins are not safe from .... by foxes and wild dogs.

9 Write a word from the text to match the meaning.

thought or plan of action ....

Circle the word on each line that does **not** belong.

10 begun, hatched, concluded, started

11 reminded, remembered, suggested, hinted

Grammar

12 Complete the sentence with an adjective from the text.

Swampy Marsh kept .... chickens.

13 Which tense is the underlined verb in this sentence?

It is time for the two dogs to retire.

....

14 Write an adverb from the text to tell **how**.

The idea was introduced

.... in 2006.

15 Choose a conjunction from the box to complete the sentence correctly.

and	so	but	because	or

Have you visited Middle Island .... not?

Punctuation

16 Circle the sentence that is punctuated correctly.

A Maremmas guard stock, sheep, chickens and, now, penguins!

B Maremmas guard stock sheep, chickens and now, penguins!

C Maremmas guard stock, sheep chickens and now, penguins.

Rewrite each sentence correctly.

17 Maremmas are native to Italy?

....

....

18 'Id love to see a baby maremma.'

....

....

....

Reading and Comprehension

Write an adjective from the box in each space.

pretty	blue	eight	old	hairy	white	baby

1 The spider in our bathroom had ____________ ____________ legs.

2 The ____________ penguin watched its mother waddle towards the clear, ____________ water.

3 'In the ____________ days,' said Mary's grandmother, 'our TV showed black and ____________ pictures. They often used pictures of women in ____________ aprons in their ads.'

Write a verb from the box in each space.

wish	swallow	destroy	got	found	finished	surprise	remember	cook

4 Be careful not to ____________ my project. I only ____________ it yesterday.

5 Mum said to ____________ you a happy birthday and tell you not to ____________ your lemonade too quickly!

6 Our survey ____________ that pizza is most people's favourite food. It isn't hard to ____________ at home so I'm going to ____________ my parents with pizza tonight.

7 I can't ____________ how that clock ____________ inside the crocodile.

Spelling

The spelling mistakes in these sentences have been circled. Write the correct spelling on the lines.

8 I am eight (yeers) old. ____________

9 Do you get (board) easily? ____________

10 I love being told fairy (tails). ____________

11 My brother can be a terrible (newsance). ____________

12 What did you do at the (weakend)? ____________

13 Have you seen the latest (advertisment) for bottled water? ____________

14 The penguins need to be (garded) from foxes. ____________

15 It is a matter for the (cowncil). ____________

Vocabulary

16 Circle the correct word in the brackets.

Will you (weight / wait) for me, please?

17 Circle the word that is opposite in meaning to the underlined word.

We will <u>probably</u> go to the Barrier Reef for our holidays.

possibly maybe definitely likely

18 Circle the word that is closest in meaning to the underlined word.

Captain Hook <u>stared</u> angrily at the crocodile as it came closer.

glanced glared peered looked

Grammar

19 Add an adjective to the sentence.

Daddy long-legs are ______________________ spiders.

20 Add a past-tense relating (being) verb to the sentence.

Yesterday at the park, they ______________________ afraid the ants would bite them.

21 Add an adverb to tell **how**.

We have to leave for the airport soon so pack your case ______________________, please.

22 Add a conjunction to the sentence.

The teacher said, 'You won't need your lunch ______________________ we will eat at the gallery.'

Punctuation

Rewrite each sentence correctly.

23 'shed love to visit japan'

____

____

24 do they make good guard dogs asked the farmer.

____

____

25 'dont swim there because there are crocodiles in the water'

____

____

Reading

Fee fi fo fum

Jack's mother knew they must get money for food. She sent Jack to town to sell their cow. A passing farmer offered Jack a handful of good luck beans in exchange for the cow.

'You silly boy,' said Jack's mother angrily, throwing the beans out of the window.

In a few days the beans grew sky-high. Being an adventurous person, Jack climbed a beanstalk. He came to a castle where an enormous giant was counting his money.

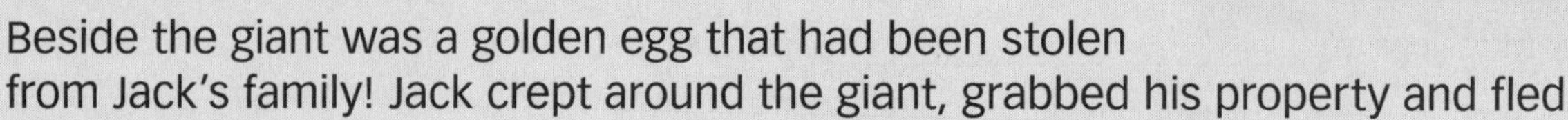

Beside the giant was a golden egg that had been stolen from Jack's family! Jack crept around the giant, grabbed his property and fled.

'Fee fi fo fum, I eat children, yum, yum, yum,' bellowed the giant. He chased swiftly after Jack. Jack got to the ground first, grabbed an axe and immediately cut down the beanstalks. That was the end of the giant and his wicked ways.

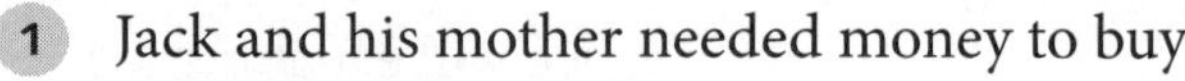

1 Jack and his mother needed money to buy
- **A** beans.
- **B** a cow.
- **C** a golden egg.
- **D** food.

2 What did Jack's mother do with the beans?
- **A** threw them out of the window
- **B** gave them to the farmer
- **C** planted them
- **D** ate them for dinner

3 How high did the beans grow?
- **A** very high
- **B** sky-high
- **C** quite high
- **D** enormously high

4 Why does Jack's mother call him a silly boy?
- **A** He'd talked to a stranger.
- **B** He'd sold the cow.
- **C** He'd accepted less than the cow was worth.
- **D** He'd had too much fun.

5 The giant bellowed 'Fee Fi Fo Fum' to
- **A** amuse Jack.
- **B** scare his neighbours.
- **C** soothe Jack.
- **D** scare Jack.

6 How does Jack save his family from starvation?
- **A** by selling the cow
- **B** by climbing the beanstalk
- **C** by rescuing the golden egg
- **D** by getting home quickly

NAPLAN-STYLE 3 CONVENTIONS OF LANGUAGE TEST

Spelling

The spelling mistakes in these sentences have been underlined. Write the correct spelling on the lines.

1 How much munney does that cost? ______________________

2 He offerred Jack some good luck beans. ______________________

3 The beans grew into very tall beanstorks. ______________________

4 Jack grabbed the axe imedeately. ______________________

Vocabulary

5 Which word means **bellowed**?

A blew B whistled C shouted D whimpered

6 Which word does **not** belong?

A borrowed B pinched C robbed D stole

7 Which word does **not** belong?

A bold B brave C fearful D adventurous

Grammar

8 Which word describes the giant?

A wicked B adventurous C daring D lazy

9 Which word from the text tells **when** Jack cut down the beanstalks?

____

10 Which word from the text tells **how** the giant chased after Jack?

____

Punctuation

11 Which sentence is punctuated correctly?

A 'Thank you my son. You've saved us' said his mother.
B 'Thank you my son.' 'You've saved us,' said his mother.
C 'Thank you my son. Youve saved us!' said his mother.
D 'Thank you my son. You've saved us!' said his mother.

12 Which sentence is punctuated correctly?

A 'How clever do you think Jack was' asked the teacher.
B I asked, 'Did the goose lay the golden egg?'
C jack's mother was furious with him.
D The giants words were very frightening.

Caterpillars

The caterpillar is an insect. It has a long, soft body. There are three parts —head, thorax and abdomen. Even though there are twelve eyelets on its head, it doesn't see well.

Like all insects it has three pairs of legs. It also has up to five pairs of false legs, stubby bumps called prolegs. These help it to hold on to plant surfaces and to climb. There are around 4000 muscles in a caterpillar's body—far more than humans have.

A caterpillar spends a lot of time hungrily eating leaves. Some caterpillars eat 27 000 times their body weight during the eating phase in their lives. They need to eat a lot in order to change into butterflies and to develop their eggs.

After two or three weeks the caterpillar stops eating and spins a cocoon. It hangs on a stick or tree. After around seven days it leaves the cocoon as a butterfly.

1. What shape are caterpillars' bodies?
   - **A** long
   - **B** fat
   - **C** short
   - **D** hard

2. How do caterpillars spend a lot of their time?
   - **A** sleeping
   - **B** eating
   - **C** flying
   - **D** thinking

3. How many pairs of legs does a caterpillar have?
   - **A** two
   - **B** three
   - **C** four
   - **D** five

4. Why might you think a caterpillar wasn't an insect?
   - **A** It appears to have more than three pairs of legs.
   - **B** It turns into a butterfly.
   - **C** It looks like a silkworm.
   - **D** It doesn't have wings.

5. What does a butterfly's egg turn into?
   - **A** a plant
   - **B** a cocoon
   - **C** a frog
   - **D** a caterpillar

6. What is unusual about the caterpillar's life cycle?
   - **A** It has a lot of muscles.
   - **B** It spins a cocoon.
   - **C** It changes into something completely different.
   - **D** It has twelve eyelets.

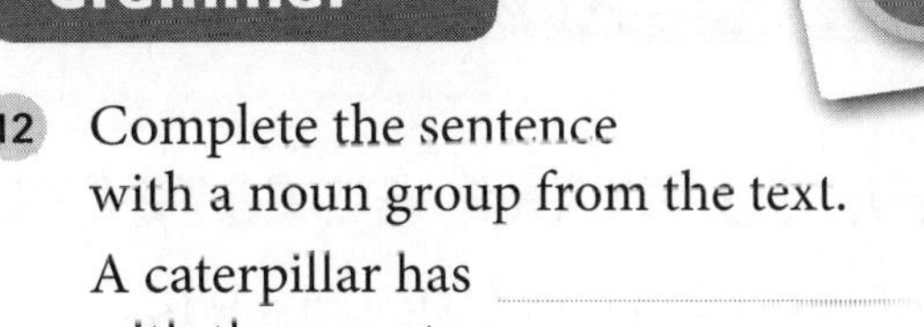

Spelling

Rewrite the misspelt words.

1 That catterpilar is green with black marks.

2 How many mussles do humans have?

3 My wait is much greater than an insect's.

4 There is a coocoon hanging on that branch.

5 Change the first letter of **bumps** to make three new words.

Vocabulary

Circle the word that has the nearest meaning to the underlined word.

6 Its prolegs are short and stubby.

A lanky B tiny
C thick D skimpy

7 Caterpillars are always eating.

A munching B biting
C dining D snacking

8 Add a word from the text to the sentence.

Caterpillars eat many times more than their body ________.

9 Write a word from the text to match the meaning.

the outside or uppermost layers

Circle the word on each line that does **not** belong.

10 false, fake, real, untrue

11 stage, phase, period, whole

Grammar

12 Complete the sentence with a noun group from the text.

A caterpillar has ________ with three parts.

13 Complete the sentence with a sensing verb from the text.

Caterpillars don't ________ clearly out of their eyelets.

14 Write an adverb from the text to tell **how**.

Caterpillars are always eating ________.

15 Choose a conjunction from the box to complete the sentence correctly.

and	so	but	because	or

A caterpillar is an insect ________ it doesn't look like an insect.

Punctuation

16 Circle the sentence that is punctuated correctly.

A All insects have a head thorax and abdomen

B All insects have a head, thorax and abdomen.

C All insects have a head thorax and abdomen.

Rewrite each sentence correctly.

17 She saw a cocoon, hanging from a branch.

18 'Do you remember that book with holes in the pages!

Reading and Comprehension

How to make a scarecrow

Scarecrows are used to scare birds away from crops. You can make one easily.

You'll need:

two poles—one longer than the other
jacket, pants and belt, pillowcase, hat
marker pens
stuffing (e.g. straw, rags)
attaching equipment (e.g. string, wire, cotton, needle, glue, hammer and nails, screws and screwdriver, safety pins)

Method:

Place the long pole vertically. About a head's length down, attach the shorter pole horizontally.

Put the shirt onto the wooden structure using the horizontal pole for the arms. Tie the arm ends together. Stuff the shirt.

Make a hole in the seat of the pants and attach to the bottom of the shirt. Push the stuffing through the legs. Tie the cuffs. Add a belt.

Make a head by half filling a pillowcase with stuffing. Pin the bottom but leave a hole. Press the head on to the vertical pole and tie it on. Draw a cheery face. Glue on some straw for hair. Add a hat.

1. How many poles do you need?
   - **A** two
   - **B** four
   - **C** six
   - **D** eight

2. The long pole is placed
   - **A** horizontally.
   - **B** upside down.
   - **C** vertically.
   - **D** back the front.

3. The stuffing can be made from
   - **A** string.
   - **B** wire.
   - **C** glue.
   - **D** rags.

4. You stuff the shirt and pants to
   - **A** get rid of old rags.
   - **B** create the shape of a body.
   - **C** make a waist for the scarecrow.
   - **D** make hands and feet.

5. The scarecrow in the picture has failed in its duty because
   - **A** it has buttons for eyes.
   - **B** it has too many patches.
   - **C** it has too big a smile.
   - **D** it hasn't scared the birds away.

6. Do you agree that it is easy to make a scarecrow?

Spelling

Rewrite the misspelt words.

1 You don't scair me!

2 That pole isn't the right lenth.

3 I made a whole in the pants for the pole to go through.

4 Are you going to scruw the poles together?

5 Change the first letter of **head** to make three new words.

Vocabulary

Circle the word that has the nearest meaning to the underlined word.

6 You need to attach the head to the body of the scarecrow.

A link B fasten
C knot D zip

7 She stuffed her scarecrow's clothes with leaves.

A placed B threaded
C filled D crowded

8 Add a word from the text to the sentence.
The purpose of the scarecrow is to scare birds ______.

9 Write a word from the text to match the meaning.
in at one place and out at the other ______

Circle the word on each line that does **not** belong.

10 astonish amaze frighten surprise

11 join connect link separate

Grammar

12 Complete the sentence with a noun group from the text.
Hang the shirt onto
______.

13 Complete the sentence with an action (doing) verb from the text.
He used safety pins to ______ the bottom of the pillowcase.

14 Write an adverb from the text to tell **how**.
You can make a scarecrow
______.

15 Choose a conjunction from the box to complete the sentence correctly.

and	so	but	because	or

You could use a needle ______ thread for the job.

Punctuation

16 Circle the sentence that is punctuated correctly.

A You can use string, wire or cotton to tie up the ends.

B You can use string, wire, or cotton, to tie up the ends.

C You can use string wire, or cotton, to tie up the ends.

Rewrite each sentence correctly.

17 'Why dont you use buttons for the eyes!'

18 that scarecrow couldn't scare anything?

Reading and Comprehension

Do computers make life better?

Noah: I think computers are amazing. You can use them to find out everything.

Jasmine: Yes, but the information you find isn't always reliable. You can be tricked into believing something is true when it isn't.

Harry: I don't get tricked! The computers let you keep in touch with people who live a long way away. My best friend lives in China. We email each other and sometimes we talk on skype.

Florence: I like doing jigsaws on my computer. It makes a satisfying click when the piece fits into its space.

Jasmine: I think real jigsaws are more fun.

Harry: Just think of doing research without a computer to help you. Way too hard!

Florence: Writing stories is more fun too. When you make a mistake you can just delete it. You can easily add photos and pictures to your work. Life without computers would be dull.

1. Who says computers are amazing?
   - **A** Harry
   - **B** Noah
   - **C** Florence
   - **D** Jasmine

2. What does Florence like doing on her computer?
   - **A** emailing
   - **B** skyping
   - **C** jigsaws
   - **D** playing games

3. Who has a friend living in China?
   - **A** Harry
   - **B** Noah
   - **C** Florence
   - **D** Jasmine

4. Harry likes computers because they
   - **A** let you have fun.
   - **B** make things easier to do.
   - **C** put you in control.
   - **D** let you delete mistakes easily.

5. Who would disagree with the idea that computers make life better?
   - **A** Harry
   - **B** Noah
   - **C** Florence
   - **D** Jasmine

6. How convincing are Jasmine's comments?
   - **A** extremely
   - **B** somewhat
   - **C** not at all
   - **D** outstandingly

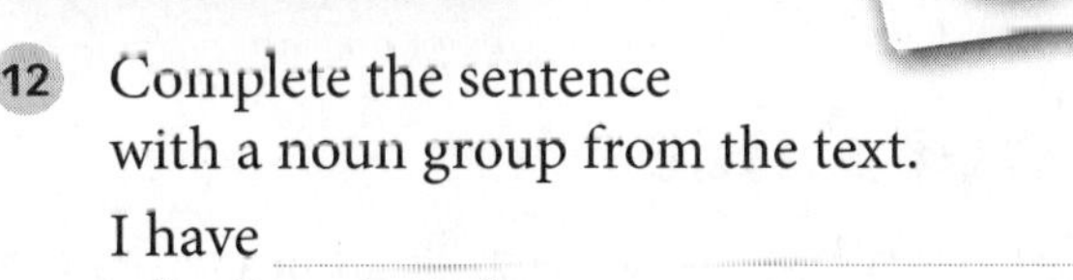

Spelling

Rewrite the misspelt words.

1 You can look up <u>everythink</u> on a computer.

2 I like searching for <u>infomation</u>.

3 This jigsaw has 25 <u>peaces</u>.

4 My <u>reserch</u> topic this term is koalas.

5 Change the first letter of **find** to make three new words.

Vocabulary

Circle the word that has the nearest meaning to the underlined word.

6 Wikipedia does not always have <u>reliable</u> information.

A useful B good
C trustworthy D honest

7 I like <u>real</u> games better than computer games.

A actual B factual
C proper D truthful

8 Add a word from the text to the sentence.
Mum lets me email my gran on her ________.

9 Write a word from the text to match the meaning.
to find out more about something

Circle the word on each line that does **not** belong.

10 correct accurate reliable uncertain

11 mistake fact error booboo

Grammar

12 Complete the sentence with a noun group from the text.
I have ________ who lives in Italy.

13 Complete the sentence with a saying verb from the text.
Sometimes we ________ on Zoom.

14 Write a prepositional phrase from the text to tell **where**.
I like playing games ________.

15 Choose a conjunction from the box to complete the sentence correctly.

and	so	but	because	or

Did you send me an email ________ a text message?

Punctuation

16 Circle the sentence that is punctuated correctly.

A She doesn't know who won the debate.
B She doesnt know who won the debate.
C She doesn't know who won the debate

Rewrite each sentence correctly.

17 'Do you agree with what I said.'

18 Stella answered 'Yes, I do.'

Reading and Comprehension

Poor Alice

Just then her head struck against the roof of the hall. In fact, she was now more than nine feet high and she at once took up the little golden key and hurried off to the garden door.

Poor Alice! It was as much as she could do, lying down on one side, to look through into the garden with one eye; but to get through was more hopeless than ever. She sat down and began to cry again.

'You ought to be ashamed of yourself,' said Alice, 'a great girl like you,' (she might well say this), 'to go on crying in this way! Stop this moment, I tell you!' But she went on all the same, shedding gallons of tears, until there was a large pool all round her, about four inches deep and reaching half down the hall.

Extract from *Alice's Adventures in Wonderland* by Lewis Carroll, 1865

John Tenniel's illustration of Alice from Project Gutenberg.

1. What did Alice's head strike?
   - A the door
   - B the fence
   - C the roof
   - D the hall

2. How did Alice lie on the ground?
   - A on her back
   - B on her side
   - C on her front
   - D on both sides

3. What surrounded Alice?
   - A a large hall
   - B a beautiful garden
   - C a pool of her own tears
   - D gallons of lake water

4. What was causing Alice's problems?
   - A She'd grown enormously.
   - B She'd drunk gallons of water.
   - C She'd shrunk in size.
   - D She was a crybaby.

5. Why did Alice talk crossly to herself?
   - A It was a habit she'd always had.
   - B There was no-one else there.
   - C She was pretending to be cross.
   - D She wanted to stop herself crying.

6. The author's attitude to Alice is mainly
   - A disapproving.
   - B sympathetic.
   - C admiring.
   - D critical.

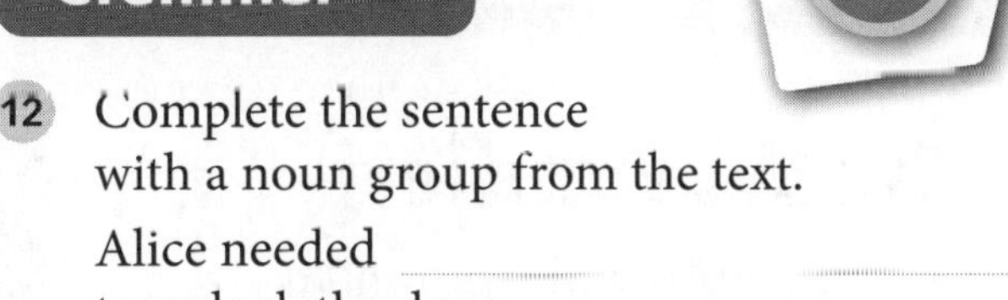

Spelling

Rewrite the misspelt words.

1 One minute she was small, the next nine feat tall!

2 Everything seemed hopless.

3 'I ort not to cry all the time,' said Alice.

4 The pool was now galons deep.

5 Change the first letter of **tears** to make three new words.

Vocabulary

Circle the word that has the nearest meaning to the underlined word.

6 She tried to stand up but her head struck the roof.

A smacked B hit
C attacked D reached

7 Now Alice was more than nine feet high!

A lofty B long
C tall D steep

8 Add a word from the text to the sentence.

It was a ______________,
not an opinion, that she'd grown so high.

9 Write a word from the text to match the meaning.

not possible to be successful

Circle the word on each line that does **not** belong.

10 pause stop continue end

11 less further more extra

Grammar

12 Complete the sentence with a noun group from the text.

Alice needed ______________
to unlock the door.

13 Complete the sentence with a sensing verb from the text.

Alice lay on her side and tried to ______________
______________ into the garden.

14 Write a prepositional phrase from the text to tell **when**.

She took up the little golden key
______________.

15 Choose a conjunction from the box to complete the sentence correctly.

and	so	but	because	or

Now the pool of tears Alice had cried was getting deeper ______________ deeper.

Punctuation

16 Circle the sentence that is punctuated correctly.

A 'I am ashamed of myself, said Alice.
B 'I am ashamed of myself' said Alice.
C 'I am ashamed of myself,' said Alice.

Rewrite each sentence correctly.

17 The tears, shed by alice soon made a deep pool

18 'Stop that crying at once.'

The Wurundjeri

Different tribes of Aboriginal people had their own customs, beliefs and languages. Within each tribe there were clans—groups of people united by kinship. Each clan had areas of land, marked off by mountains, rivers and other natural landmarks, that they cared for.

The Wurundjeri are from areas of land in south-west Melbourne. Like all Aboriginal people, the Wurundjeri clan feel a very strong connection to the land. They believe it is given to them by their spirit ancestors to use and look after. In the past, they did this by using the resources of an area then moving on. They think of themselves as belonging to the land rather than owning it.

In Aboriginal culture a totem is a natural object, plant or animal. It is a spiritual emblem. The totem of the Wurundjeri is Bunjil the eagle. In Melbourne today there is a street named Wurundjeri Way. An eagle sits silently above looking down at the city.

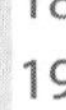

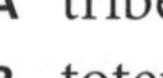

1 The Wurundjeri are a
- A tribe.
- B totem.
- C clan.
- D place.

2 The Wurundjeri believe their land is given to them by
- A totems.
- B other tribes.
- C other clans.
- D spirit ancestors.

3 Bunjil is
- A a live eagle.
- B a totem.
- C a street.
- D a building.

4 Why didn't clans stay in the same area all the time?
- A They liked to travel.
- B They thought that was boring.
- C They got itchy feet.
- D The area needed to recover its resources.

5 Aboriginal people think of the land as something
- A they want to own for themselves.
- B they are a part of.
- C that only provides shelter.
- D that they have fought for.

6 Why is there a sculpture of an eagle above Wurundjeri Way?
- A It likes to look down at the city.
- B It was put there by chance.
- C It is a symbol of the Wurundjeri people.
- D It is too heavy to move.

Spelling

Rewrite the misspelt words.

1 Each tribe has its own langwege.

2 Totems are usually plants or annimals.

3 Melbourne is a citee in Victoria.

4 Have you seen the eegle sitting on that building?

5 Change the first letter of **land** to make three new words.

Vocabulary

Circle the word that has the nearest meaning to the underlined word.

6 They lived in an area near the Yarra.
A part B spot
C circle D route

7 She felt a strong kinship with the land.
A connection B quarrel
C conflict D clash

8 Add a word from the text to the sentence.
The ______ spoke their own languages.

9 Write a word from the text to match the meaning.
usual ways of doing something ______

Circle the word on each line that does **not** belong.

10 tribes groups individuals clans

11 doubts opinions beliefs views

Grammar

12 Complete the sentence with a noun group from the text.
______ are from areas of land in south-west Melbourne.

13 Complete the sentence with a relating (being) verb from the text.
In Aboriginal culture, a totem ______ a spiritual emblem.

14 Write an adverb from the text to tell **how**.
The eagle sits there ______ watching the city below.

15 Choose a conjunction from the box to complete the sentence correctly.

and	so	but	because	or

'We are part of the land ______ the land is part of us.'

Punctuation

16 Circle the sentence that is punctuated correctly.
A Boundaries were marked by mountains rivers and other landmarks.
B Boundaries were marked by mountains, rivers and other landmarks.
C Boundaries were marked by mountains, rivers, and other, landmarks.

Rewrite each sentence correctly.

17 'have you seen Bunjil the eagle in Melbourne'

18 Aboriginal people share many beliefs!

Reading and Comprehension

What is a census?

A census involves counting the number of people in a country, city or town and collecting information about them.

The first national census in Australia collected information about every single person and their dwellings on 2 April 1911. Since 1961, the census has been taken every five years. It is compulsory for each household to answer the questions on the census.

Up until 2016, paper censuses were taken to, and collected from, every household. In 2016, people were asked to fill in the census online for the very first time.

There are questions about name, age, birth, occupation, religion, languages, and so on. This information is then added together and reported as numbers and amounts (statistics). It provides a picture of who makes up the Australian population, where they live, what they are doing, their religious beliefs, and so on at that moment in time.

Governments use these findings to plan services such as transport, housing, education and hospitals.

1. Since 1961, there has been a census in Australia every
   - **A** year.
   - **B** two years.
   - **C** five years.
   - **D** ten years.

2. When was the first time the census could be done online?
   - **A** 1911
   - **B** 1961
   - **C** 2011
   - **D** 2016

3. Filling in the census is
   - **A** compulsory.
   - **B** a matter of choice.
   - **C** voluntary.
   - **D** encouraged.

4. The picture represents
   - **A** three males and three females.
   - **B** four males and two females.
   - **C** five males and one female.
   - **D** two males and four females.

5. If you compare the 1911 and 2011 census results you are likely to see
   - **A** very little change.
   - **B** enormous change.
   - **C** some change.
   - **D** no change.

6. Why does the government want the census to be filled in online?

   ....

   ....

   ....

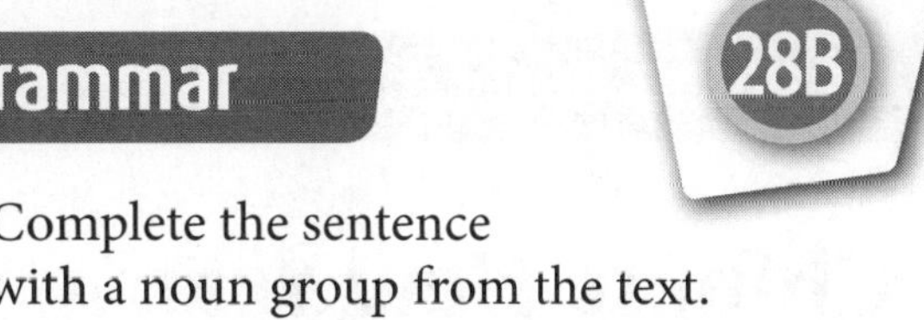

Spelling

Rewrite the misspelt words.

1 Mum and Dad filled in the sensus online this year.

2 Do you know how many peeple live in Darwin now?

3 There are a lot of qestions to answer on the form.

4 Is it compulsery to fill in the census?

5 Change the first letter of **fill** to make three new words.

Vocabulary

Circle the word that has the nearest meaning to the underlined word.

6 Mum's occupation is teaching.

A job B trade
C craft D pastime

7 We filled in information about our family carefully.

A clues B tips
C facts D ideas

8 Add a word from the text to the sentence.

In 1911 there was a ______ census in Australia.

9 Write a word from the text to match the meaning.

information in the form of numbers and amounts ______

Circle the word on each line that does **not** belong.

10 collect gather separate compile

11 single double sole only

Grammar

12 Complete the sentence with a noun group from the text.

Before 2016, ______ were delivered to every household.

13 Complete the sentence with a relating (being) verb from the text.

There ______ questions about many different things on a census.

14 Write a prepositional phrase from the text to tell **when**.

The 1911 census was held ______.

15 Choose a conjunction from the box to complete the sentence correctly.

and	so	but	because	or

Families can now fill in the census on paper ______ online.

Punctuation

16 Circle the sentence that is punctuated correctly.

A The census was taken, on 9 August 2016.
B 'The census was taken on 9 August 2016.
C The census was taken on 9 August 2016.

Rewrite each sentence correctly.

17 People fill in the census, with paper and pen.

18 Until 2016 the census was not filled in online!

Reading and Comprehension

Chinese New Year

Hi Amy

You asked me to tell you how we celebrate Chinese New Year here. We always have a holiday at this time. It is our Spring Festival. The celebrations last for fifteen days. They end with the Lantern Festival when children carry paper lanterns, often in the shape of animals, to the temples.

The festival is held to honour deities and ancestors. It has been celebrated in China for centuries. Today, many places with a Chinese population, such as Thailand, Cambodia, Indonesia, Malaysia and Australia, hold similar celebrations.

We clean our house from top to bottom to make room for bad luck to leave and good luck to enter. We decorate the windows and doors with pretty, red paper-cutouts. Sometimes we light firecrackers and join in the Dragon Parade. On the front of this postcard you can see a picture of a street in Beijing decorated with Chinese New Year ornaments. Hope your project goes well.

With love
Auntie Changchang

1. What do the children carry during the Lantern festival?
   - **A** ornaments
   - **B** animals
   - **C** paper lanterns
   - **D** decorations

2. In which season is the Chinese New Year Festival held?
   - **A** spring
   - **B** summer
   - **C** autumn
   - **D** winter

3. How long does the Festival last?
   - **A** one day
   - **B** centuries
   - **C** fifteen days
   - **D** one week

4. Where does Auntie Changchang live?
   - **A** Malaysia
   - **B** Indonesia
   - **C** China
   - **D** Australia

5. Why does Amy ask her aunt for information about Chinese New Year?
   - **A** for a school project
   - **B** She wants to celebrate it.
   - **C** She is going to a Chinese New Year celebration.
   - **D** She is curious.

6. Auntie Changchang's information sounds
   - **A** questionable.
   - **B** fishy.
   - **C** unlikely.
   - **D** reliable.

Spelling

Rewrite the misspelt words.

1 Is your lantern made of papper?

2 I'm going to the sellabrations tonight!

3 Australia has a smaller poppulation than China.

4 There were many families at the Draggon Parade.

5 Change the first letter of **light** to make three new words.

Vocabulary

Circle the word that has the nearest meaning to the underlined word.

6 The Festival honours our ancestors.

A notices **B** celebrates
C watches **D** trusts

7 The lantern was in the shape of an animal.

A form **B** pattern
C frame **D** shadow

8 Add a word from the text to the sentence.

Most of the ornaments used to ______ our houses are red.

9 Write a word from the text to match the meaning.

the number of people living in a country, town or other area ______

Circle the word on each line that does **not** belong.

10 pretty attractive disagreeable delightful

11 ancestors forefathers relatives friends

Grammar

12 Complete the sentence with a noun group from the text.

If you add ______ to the windows and doors, it will look cheerful.

13 Complete the sentence with an action (doing) verb from the text.

How do you ______ New Year's Day in your country?

14 Write a prepositional phrase from the text to tell **how**.

At Chinese New Year we clean our house ______.

15 Choose a conjunction from the box to complete the sentence correctly.

and	so	but	because	or

We celebrate Chinese New Year ______ we can honour our deities and ancestors.

Punctuation

16 Circle the sentence that is punctuated correctly.

A The decorations are red, yellow, and, white.
B The decorations are red, yellow and white.
C The decorations are red yellow and white.

Rewrite each sentence correctly.

17 Auntie changchang sent me a postcard?

18 I hope I did well, in my project.

Reading and Comprehension

Home at last!

Both men waited for the moment when the Kangaroo should be seen again.

The next instant the Kangaroo bounded out of the Bush into the open paddock. Swift as lightning up went the cruel gun, but, as it exploded with a terrible report, the man, Jack, struck it upwards, and the fatal bullet lodged in the branch of a tall gum tree.

Frank Mahony's illustration for *Dot and the Kangaroo* from Project Gutenberg.

'Great Scott!' exclaimed Jack, pointing at the Kangaroo.

'Dot!' cried her father, dropping his gun, and stumbling blindly forward with outstretched arms, towards his little girl, who had just tumbled out of the Kangaroo's pouch in her hurry to reach her father …

And all the time the good Kangaroo sat up on her haunches, still panting with fear from the sound of the gun, and a little afraid to stay, yet so interested in all the excitement and delight, that she couldn't make up her mind to hop away.

An extract from *Dot and the Kangaroo* by Edith Pedley, 1899

1. Where did the bullet lodge?
   - **A** in the kangaroo
   - **B** in Dot
   - **C** in Jack
   - **D** in the gum tree

2. Who said, 'Great Scott!'?
   - **A** Dot
   - **B** Jack
   - **C** the Kangaroo
   - **D** Dot's father

3. Where had Dot just been?
   - **A** in a gum tree
   - **B** in a bush
   - **C** in the Kangaroo's pouch
   - **D** in the house

4. What had Dot's father meant to do?
   - **A** frighten Jack
   - **B** frighten the Kangaroo
   - **C** shoot the gum tree
   - **D** shoot the Kangaroo

5. Dot's return makes her father feel
   - **A** upset.
   - **B** sad.
   - **C** delighted.
   - **D** afraid.

6. What is the author's attitude to the shooting attempt?
   - **A** disapproval
   - **B** approval
   - **C** surprise
   - **D** amusement

Spelling

Rewrite the misspelt words.

1 The Kangaroo bownded towards the paddock.

....

2 The shooting made a terrible noyse.

....

3 Dot had kept warm in the Kangaroo's powch.

....

4 The animals were panting with feer.

....

5 Change the first letter of **seen** to make three new words.

....

....

....

Vocabulary

Circle the word that has the nearest meaning to the underlined word.

6 Dot tumbled from the Kangaroo's pouch to the ground.

A sagged B plunged
C flopped D toppled

7 The shot could have been fatal.

A dreadful B harmful
C deadly D serious

8 Add a word from the text to the sentence.

Quick as ...., he pushed the gun away.

9 Write a word from the text to match the meaning.

causing death ....

Circle the word on each line that does **not** belong.

10 afraid frightened brave scared

11 silence sound noise din

Grammar

12 Complete the sentence with a noun group from the text.

.... bounded into the open paddock.

13 Complete the sentence with a saying verb from the text.

'Dot!', ... her father in despair.

14 Write an adverb from the text to tell **how**.

Dot's father stumbled .... towards his little girl.

15 Choose a conjunction from the box to complete the sentence correctly.

and	so	but	because	or

The word 'kangaroo' doesn't usually have a capital letter .... it does in this story.

Punctuation

16 Circle the sentence that is punctuated correctly.

A 'Oh no!' shouted Dots dad.
B 'Oh no' shouted Dot's dad.
C 'Oh no!' shouted Dot's dad.

Rewrite each sentence correctly.

17 The Kangaroo watched Dot run, to her father?

....

....

....

18 'help!' shouted Jack.

....

....

....

Reading and Comprehension

Underline the noun group in each sentence.

1 Was there a census taken in 2016?

2 I saw a hairy, green caterpillar over there.

3 She made the pretty decorations.

Write a word from the box in each space.

butterfly	ashamed	crops	cocoon	home	used	moment	comfortably

4 Scarecrows are ______________ by farmers to scare away birds from their ______________.

5 After two or three weeks the caterpillar stops eating and spins a ______________. It hangs on a stick or tree. After around seven days the caterpillar leaves as a ______________.

6 'You ought to be ______________ of yourself,' said Alice, 'a great girl like you,' (she might well say this), 'to go on crying in this way! Stop this ______________, I tell you!'

7 Dot rode along ______________ in the Kangaroo's pouch. She was looking forward to being back ______________ again.

Spelling

The spelling mistakes in these sentences have been circled. Write the correct spelling on the lines.

8 I use my computer to send (emales). ______________

9 His sculptures were mainly of (annimals). ______________

10 You need to leave a (whole) for the neck of the scarecrow. ______________

11 It is (crewel) to behave like that. ______________

12 Write your answers on the (paiper) on your desk. ______________

13 I feel (hopless) because I can't do anything to help. ______________

14 People from different countries enjoyed the (sellabration). ______________

15 The census counts the whole (poppulashion). ______________

Vocabulary

16 Circle the correct word in the brackets.
He (new / knew) how to make a scarecrow.

17 Circle the word that means the opposite of **opinion**.
view fact thought attitude

Grammar

18 Add a noun group to the sentence.
______________________________ of the caterpillar is long and soft.

19 Add a relating (being) verb to the sentence.
There ______________________________ a room full of computers at our school.

20 Add a prepositional phrase to tell **where**.
We keep our ice-cream ____.

21 Add a conjunction to the sentence.
I don't like that story ______________________________ it is too scary.

22 Add a conjunction to the sentence.
We could either go to the movies ______________________________ go skating.

Punctuation

Rewrite each sentence correctly.

23 scarecrows are fun to make

____

____

24 'Why dont you disappear' asked Alice.

____

____

25 'Look out.' Jack yelled

____

____

Reading

NAPLAN-STYLE 4 READING TEST

Our holiday in Melbourne

    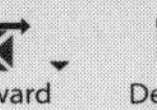    

Back Compose Reply Reply all Forward Delete Move Print Mark More

Dear Gran

You'll never guess what I saw yesterday! We were driving into Melbourne from the airport and there, up high, looking out over the city, was Bunjil the eagle. I remember you telling me about him. Dad says he is more than 20 metres high. I think he has a friendly, wise spirit.

Tomorrow we are going to see an exhibition of other sculptures made by Bruce Armstrong. I saw pictures of some of them, including Bunjil, in an advertisement at our hotel. There are two huge animals that have been carefully carved from enormous red river gum trees. They look like rhinos or maybe fat crocodiles.

Our whole family went around the city circle on a free tourist tram. They go every 12 minutes and you can get on and off when you choose. We stopped by the murky, brown Yarra for lunch ☺. See you soon.

Love

Chilli

1 Chilli's family travelled around the city circle on a

- A plane.
- B taxi.
- C tram.
- D car.

2 Who told Chilli about Bunjil the eagle?

- A her dad
- B Bruce Armstrong
- C her gran
- D her family

3 Where did the family stop for lunch?

- A the Yarra
- B the airport
- C the gallery
- D the hotel

4 Why is Chilli in Melbourne?

- A She's shopping for her gran.
- B Her parents have work.
- C She was invited by Bruce Armstrong.
- D Her family is having a holiday.

5 Why does Chilli add a smiley face to her comment about the Yarra?

- A to show she isn't too serious
- B her gran likes smileys
- C because she dislikes the Yarra
- D to show off her computer skills

6 Chilli's relationship with her gran is

- A awkward.
- B loving.
- C up and down.
- D distant.

NAPLAN-STYLE 4 CONVENTIONS OF LANGUAGE TEST

Spelling

The spelling mistakes in these sentences have been underlined. Write the correct spelling on the lines.

1 Gran couldn't <u>gess</u> what I'd seen. ______________________

2 It was a splendid <u>eegle</u>. ______________________

3 We went to see the sculptures because of the <u>advertisment</u>. ______________________

4 The carved animals are <u>enoremus</u>! ______________________

Vocabulary

5 Which word means **exhibition**?

A carnival B fair C display D pictures

6 Which word does **not** belong?

A big B large C short D enormous

7 Which word does **not** belong?

A clever B sensible C smart D unwise

Grammar

8 Which noun from the text completes the noun group?

Our whole ______________ went on a tourist tram.

9 Which verb completes the sentence correctly?

Gran ______________ Melbourne last year.

A watched B followed C visited D stopped

10 Which word completes the sentence to tell **how**?

The wood had to be carved ______________ in case it splintered.

A quickly B carefully C briskly D cheerfully

Punctuation

11 Which sentence is punctuated correctly?

A Bruce armstrong is a well-known australian sculptor.
B Bruce Armstrong is a well-known australian sculptor.
C Bruce Armstrong is a well-known Australian sculptor.

12 Which sentence is punctuated correctly?

A Chilli said, 'Did you see Bunjil?'
B Have you ever been to Melbourne?' asked Chilli.
C The Yarra is an important river in melbourne.

Reprinted 2019, 2020, 2021, 2022

Updated in 2024 for the NSW Curriculum and Australian Curriculum Version 9.0 changes

Reprinted 2025

ISBN 978 1 74125 611 6

Pascal Press
PO Box 250
Glebe NSW 2037
www.pascalpress.com.au

Publisher: Vivienne Joannou
Project editors: Rosemary Peers and Mark Dixon
Edited by Rosemary Peers and Mark Dixon
Answers checked by Glenda Walsh
Proofread by Barbara Bessant
Cover and page design by Kim Webber
Typeset by Julianne Billington (lj Design) and Leanne Richters (Grizzly Graphics)
Printed by Vivar Printing/Green Giant Press